# THE CREATIVE VEGETARIAN

# THE CREATIVE VEGETARIAN

**Sally and David Clare**

PRISM PRESS

First published in Australasia in 1987 by
Nature & Health Books.
This edition published in Great Britain by
Prism Press, 2 South Street, Bridport,
Dorset DT6 3NQ, England
and distributed in the United States of America by
the Avery Publishing Group Inc., 350 Thorens Avenue,
Garden City Park,
New York 11040.

ISBN 1 85327 000 8

616.5

Series editor: Nevill Drury
Editor: Penny Walker
Design: Craig Peterson

Typeset by Setila Type Studios, Sydney
Printed in Australia by The Book Printer

# CONTENTS

A creative cookbook
from The Fernery
to all our friends ...

The intention of this book is to stimulate the creative power that lies within us all, and to bring it forth in the realm of good food. We see the preparation, presentation and enjoyment of natural foods as a source of learning, and a clear step towards personal and global health.

It seems that we as humans, are a medium for creation. Through us, all things hang in the balance. We choose the possibility of our future just by being how we are. Our hope is that we be true to that which is latent in all of us. That which makes us one... our own humanity.

For a better future now...

We choose...
We have the power to create.

# ABOUT THE FERNERY

Our idea to open a vegetarian restaurant began as a hopeful daydream Sally and I shared while backpacking through Europe in early 1981. At that time we ate mostly vegetarian through circumstance rather than choice. Our lean budget dictated a staple diet of fruit, bread, cheese, nuts and olives, all of which we'd buy from the street markets. The only occasions on which we did eat meat was when staying with people we'd met.

It was a newfound friend who took us out to our first vegetarian restaurant. This was a small converted house in Hampstead, north of London, called Earth Exchange. We were so impressed with the food and the atmosphere there that from that night on we began to talk about the possibililty of establishing our own little restaurant.

During the rest of our travels we discovered other vegetarian restaurants and found ways to treat ourselves to more of this wonderful cuisine. The more we realised what could be done with vegetable cookery the more we began to question the need for meat on our plate at all.

Our ideas were changing and we pursued our interest in vegetarian food, it became clear to us that this was an ideal diet.

We understood that to adopt a fleshless diet in a meat-eating society would take a strong commitment and made this together one morning like a shared realisation.

It was a full four years from the time of our return to Sydney until the opportunity to actually start a vegetarian restaurant arose. Sally was the driving force behind the venture. Having put most of her ideas together from first-hand experience in other restaurants and a room full of vegetarian cookery books, she followed through on a strong desire to do it her way.

The doors of The Fernery were opened on 6 March 1985 with Sally at the helm. Her main aim in the restaurant has been to prepare innovative, wholesome vegetarian food that looks good, tastes great and most important of all, allows people to see what can be done with vegetable cookery and its presentation. We also made it our intention to create an atmosphere which was elegant, yet relaxed and comfortable with plenty of greenery and soft ambient music.

Since opening we have allowed the restaurant to grow like the ferns which complement its name. Not so much in size or numbers, but more in terms of the subtle changes and new innovations which we find keeps our little place fresh and interesting for those who frequent it. Our customers come from all walks of life, from alternative to mainstream, young and old alike. It seems that vegetarianism is expanding across all social barriers as more and more people discover its virtues. We also find that many people come in to try vegetarian food for the first time, and it is here that we really feel that we can make an impact, just as we were once nudged onto the path back in London.

# POINTS OF VIEW

There are many points of view to consider when discussing the reasons for being a vegetarian. These range widely in topic and conviction. For some vegetarianism is part of their religious beliefs, while for others it is a simple love of animals which has caused them to choose a vegetarian diet. There are many moral reasons for not eating meat, and more recently there has been an abundance of medical research which fully supports the health improvement aspects of vegetarianism. Whatever the reasons behind the choice, it is clear that there are many people at this point in time who are consciously choosing to live on a diet that does not include the flesh of our fellow creatures. In the next few pages we will look at some of the many reasons for choosing a vegetarian diet, in an attempt to create an overview of where this shift in our lives may take us.

Probably the oldest reasons for adhering to a vegetarian diet are found in ancient texts and scriptures which have the power to touch us deeply with their timeless wisdom. Many religious and spiritual groups which have grown from these writings support the ideal of vegetarianism. It is seen as a step towards an appreciation of life and creation that is naturally conducive to spiritual growth. Hindus, Buddhists, Krishnas, Taoists, Seventh Day Adventists and many other groups are amongst those who believe that spiritual progress requires peace and harmony with the environment, with animals, and with each other. In a nutshell, vegetarianism is a way of respecting and preserving life as a precious gift from God.

In ancient Hebrew scriptures, which make up the Book of Genesis in the Old Testament, God says to Adam on the sixth day of creation, 'I have given you every herb bearing seed, which is upon the face of all the earth, and every tree, in that which is the fruit of a tree yielding seed; to you it shall be for meat'(Genesis 2:29). God goes on to say, 'And to every beast of the earth, and to every fowl of the air, and to everything that creepeth upon the earth, wherein there is life, I have given every green herb for meat...'(Genesis 2:30). It is clear that in God's divine plan there was no need to kill for food, even among the animal kingdom. Both humans and beasts were to be herbivorous and live side by side in peace. This is further mentioned in Isaiah where God describes His plan for 'new heavens and a new earth'. 'The wolf and the lamb shall feed together, and the lion shall eat straw like the bullock: and dust shall be the serpent's meat. They shall not hurt nor destroy in all my holy mountain, saith the Lord.'(Isaiah 65:25) Even after the great flood, when God gives Noah permission to use the animals for food, He starts by saying 'And the fear of you and the dread of you shall be upon every beast of the earth'. It seems that even though meat consumption was permitted by God, it was far from His ideal. In Isaiah is written 'He that killeth an ox is as if he slew a man'(Isaiah 66:3). Strong words, but very clear for those who will listen.

In the early days of Christianity there were many sects that opposed meat-eating. St Jerome, Clement of Alexandria, St John, Chrysostom, St Francis and St Benedict were all advocates of a non-violent diet. On the other side of the globe, Buddha spread the doctrine of non-violence or 'ahisma' at a time when animal slaughter was widespread. As a result of his devoted work we now see the largest concentration of vegetarians in the world living in India and the Eastern countries that follow his teachings. This same theme is present in many of the Eastern religions that are now gaining acceptance in the West. Members of the Hare Krishna movement, who base their teachings on the ancient Vedic scriptures of India, believe that while Man continues to slaughter animals, there will always be war and violence on our planet as this is a direct karmic consequence of the carnage we perpetrate daily on the animal kingdom. They see that world peace and harmony is unattainable until we put an end to this unnatural practice.

Another strong and very old aspect of vegetarianism is the moral question. Should we kill and eat any moving creature when we have the intelligence, the means and the inner feelings to choose otherwise. Many great minds in the past have engaged in this debate as a voice for the animals who have no say in the matter. One of the earliest known vegetarian orators was the famous Greek philosopher and mathematician Pythagoras, who said 'O my fellow men, do not defile your bodies with sinful foods . . . The earth affords a lavish supply of riches, of innocent foods, and offers you banquets which require no bloodshed or slaughter'. Some of the great men since who have shared this view and have expressed their feelings on the matter include Plato, Leonardo da Vinci, Socrates, Leo Tolstoy, Benjamin Franklin, Voltaire, Newton, Gandhi, Einstein, Darwin, Shelley, George Bernard Shaw and H. G. Wells. The list goes on and grows bigger as we approach the present times with names like Bob Dylan, Paul Newman, Shirley MacLaine, Richard Bach, William Shatner, Kate Bush, George Harrison, Paul and Linda McCartney, Annie Lennox, Donovan, Peter Gabriel, Uri Geller and Michael Jackson. The list of vegetarians includes millions of people who will never be household names, yet are equally as great in what they do best. Vegetarians are not only found among a non-conformist fringe element of society: They include people from all walks of life and all age groups.

Throughout history and right up to the present day, we can study entire cultures which have thrived on vegetarian or near-vegetarian diets. From Indian tribes in the Andes of South America and the high mountains of Mexico, through Asia, India, all through the Himalayas and parts of the Middle East there have been groups of people whose diet has been simple and in most cases totally devoid of meat, yet their vitality and longevity have amazed Westerners.

In actual fact it has only been in the last century that meat has been consumed on a large scale. This seems particularly so in modern Western society where new methods of farming, refrigeration and transport have made meat a viable and most profitable industry. In order to expand the market for meat there have been many myths perpetrated. Within a few generations it became generally accepted that man had always eaten plenty of meat and always would. It became a common belief that the protein from meat is an essential part of a well-balanced diet, and that 'men' especially needed to eat large amounts of meat to grow strong and healthy. With the increase of meat in the diet and the consequent drop in dietary fibre, came a sharp rise in the occurrence of the so-called 'degenerative' diseases such as cancer and heart disease which had previously been quite rare. Even today, with more than enough medical evidence to refute the meat myths, these beliefs continue to thrive through habit and upbringing. Despite this, however, we can see that the grip is beginning to lose its hold. Even with the aid of slick, multi-million dollar advertising campaigns by the meat industry, it is obvious that people are choosing for themselves at last.

From a physical health point of view, there are many reasons why it is not a good thing to put meat inside our bodies. As soon as an animal is killed its flesh begins the process of decay. Denatured substances called ptomaines are formed which cause rapid decomposition and putrefaction. Since the human digestive tract is about five times longer in proportion to that of natural carnivors, and has about twenty times less acid, the putrefying meat stays in the body far too long and allows many poisons from the decaying meat to be absorbed through the colon and into the body. Small pockets in the large intestine called diverticula can trap pieces of meat and hold them for many months. This is a constant source of poison and putrefaction, and a prime suspect for the occurrence of bowel cancer.

There are many contaminants which are already present in meat by the time it has reached the butcher's shop. These come under three categories, two of which are man's own doing. The first category consists of all the hormones, antibiotics and tranquillisers pumped into an animal before its death, as well as further chemicals which are used to slow putrefaction and artificially retain the colour of the meat as it decomposes. The second category is made up of accumulated poisons such as herbicides, pesticides and other pollutants ingested by the animal, which have been known to reach dangerously high levels of concentration. The third group consists of the natural contaminants which occur in meat such as lactic and uric acid, and those which occur as a result of the animal's state of terror immediately prior to its slaughter, such as adrenaline and other muscle-stimulating hormones.

Because meat has such a low fibre content it is often the cause of constipation and poor elimination, especially in conjunction with highly processed, low-fibre convenience foods. Also the high level of urea and uric acid in a meat diet places an unnatural burden on the kidneys which has been shown to lead to gout, arthritis, rheumatism and kidney disease. The high level of saturated fats associated with a meat diet has been undeniably linked to heart disease – the number one killer in Western society – yet it is almost unheard of in areas of the globe where meat is a rarity. Research has shown that a single barbequed or chargrilled steak can contain more carcinogens than several hundred cigarettes.

If we look at the planet as a global village it is not hard to see that the distribution of wealth and the sharing of natural resources is a little uneven. We blindly allow hunger to exist under the assumption that there is simply not enough to go around, yet in reality there is plenty to feed the entire population and more. This thought, together with the fact that meat production requires approximately twenty times the arable land to produce the same amount of protein and food value as a crop of soya beans, paves a clear path towards a future of plenty rather than one of artificial shortages, greed and wasteful habits.

Finally I would like to look at the 'etheric' value of what we eat. This concerns the realm of energy. When we eat there are physical sensations, chemical reactions and an interaction between the energy of the food and the energy of our body. We effectively take on this new energy as, according to the laws of physics, it can neither be created nor destroyed. Expanding on this it is easy to see that foods with a high energy level will be more stimulating for the body than foods that are dead and decomposing. This line of thought has led to the increasing popularity and availability of live foods such as alfalfa sprouts, beansprouts, wheatgrass and fresh organic fruits and vegetables. People who have taken on a diet of raw, living foods are discovering incredible results such as new levels of vitality and awareness previously unknown to them, a natural tendency towards positive and constructive thinking, a total lack of physical ailments, and incredibly fast healing times for cuts and burns. Gaining energy from living foods has been shown to set a person on a sure path to health and vitality in mind, body and spirit.

This brings me to an assessment of just where all this may be heading. It seems an increased awareness of Man's impact on his environment and the ability we all have to make a difference in the world are powerful allies of vegetarianism. Where would we be if the shift towards a vegetarian lifestyle continued to gather pace until the point where a non-violent diet and outlook became accepted as the way things are? In time we could be living in a world full of people with healthy bodies and healthy minds, where spiritual growth took place as a matter of course. Vast areas of land previously used for the rearing of animals for slaughter would be freed for farming crops, planting orchards or re-afforestation. Our world would be on the path of non-violence and more food would be available for us to share. Man may find new levels of contact with the creatures who share our planet, and a wonderful new sense of purpose in creation. It may all sound a bit heady, but just remember that many great minds in the past have shared this same idealistic dream for a planet that works for everyone and everything. Albert Einstein, one of the greatest thinkers of all time, said . . . 'It is my view that the vegetarian manner of living, by its purely physical effect on the human temperament, would most beneficially influence the lot of mankind . . .'

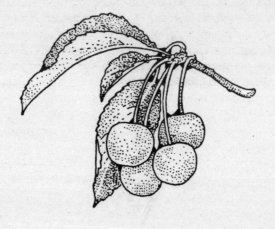

# BASIC NUTRITION

Neither Sally nor I have a formal education in nutrition; so much of what is written here is simply derived from things we have learned ourselves and the views and ideas we have shaped from them. It is by no means gospel. Since our decision to live on a meatless diet we have read many books and articles which give information on health and nutrition for vegetarians. Some of these we have found to be very helpful and informative. Others we have found to be extremely rigid and uninspiring, as they regimentally include everything needed in so-called balanced diet, except for one important ingredient . . . enjoyment! What we also found was that there are many different opinions on what one should or should not eat to stay healthy in body, mind and spirit. After a while we became a little disillusioned with all these rights and wrongs and their associated grey areas, and found ourselves almost unconsciously drifting back towards an ever-available selection of processed foods which provided our stomachs with little more than bulk. By looking outside for all the answers and losing interest with each new contradiction, we were slinking back into being the victims of convenience. I believe this syndrome has reclaimed many new and well-intentioned converts. When combined with all the social pressures that go against the decision to become vegetarian, there is little wonder that many people return to the convenience of having meat in their diet after a certain period without it.

If it's any help to know, what saved Sally and me from the clutches of confusion was our commitment to eating what felt right for us. This meant that we could enjoy the foods we felt like and let our own common sense guide us to a healthier diet. I should add that this is still happening for us, and the result is that over a period of time we have 'grown into' our diet as our knowledge has grown. I believe that choosing the vegetarian alternative to a conventional diet is like stepping onto a path that leads us all, at our own pace, towards a better appreciation and understanding of food and its effect on our body, as well as a deeper appreciation of life itself.

The information in the next few pages is not there to tell you what is right or wrong to eat, but rather to provide guidelines which may help you to choose what is right for you. It is our belief that common sense will lead us all to a healthier diet if we are willing, and that the rate of change at which this occurs will be directly proportional to our needs.

## Protein

Of all the aspects of vegetarianism, its protein content is probably the most talked about and least understood. There is a strong myth which lives among many who say that humans need to consume plenty of good protein (usually meaning fish, meat, eggs, dairy products, etc.) in order to build a strong and healthy body. What is generally not known is that large amounts of protein, or the essential amino acids required by the body to build protein, are present in many of the vegetables, nuts and grains that are generally already in our everyday diet. As more research is being done it seems the recommended daily intake of protein is dropping steadily to a point where it is no longer a matter of concern to anyone with a reasonably varied vegetarian or vegan diet. Actual cases of protein deficiency are rare, and are mostly attributed to an extreme diet which shows little common sense. If you are concerned about protein intake, there is a simple guideline put forward by Francis Moore Lappe in her book *Diet for a Small Planet*. This is called protein complementation and is based on the idea of combining at least two protein sources in the one meal to ensure an adequate balance of essential amino acids for the body to build its own protein: for example, nuts and legumes, grains and nuts, or legumes and seeds.

With a basic knowledge of protein complementation and a common-sense approach to variation in the diet, there is little need to be concerned over adequate protein intake. If you have recently given away meat I would say the best approach is to wean the body from excessive protein intake over a period of time by a gradual process of elimination and substitution. The chain may look something like this: red meat, poultry, seafood, eggs, dairy products, legumes, nuts, grains, seeds and vegetables.

### Vitamin B12

This is another hot topic in the vegetarian debate. Vitamin B12 is only required in very small amounts, but is nevertheless most essential for the body's wellbeing. The centre of debate hinges on the fact that there are few known sources of B12 in the plant kingdom, therefore a diet which does not include at least some animal products must be unnatural if artificial supplementation is required. This is a valid point until we look further and find that B12 is actually heat – and water-soluble and is lost in such processes as cooking and pasteurisation anyway. This is supported by the fact that pernicious anaemia, which is said to be caused by B12 deficiency, is just as common in meat eaters as in vegetarians. Research has also shown that B12 can be stored in the liver for years, which eliminates the need for a regular source. Given now that fermented soya products and some sea vegetables are rich in this vitamin, we can see that much of the information which led to the understanding that B12 must be supplemented was, to say the least, incomplete. If you feel safer with a B12 supplement, however, it will do no harm and certainly allows for peace of mind.

### Iron

This is a most important nutrient for the body as it maintains healthy blood. Without sufficient iron in the diet we start to feel tired and lack vitality and ambition.

Sounds familiar? One of the best ways of ensuring adequate iron intake is to use cast-iron cookware. Dietary sources include green leafy vegetables, grains and soya products. Avoid refined foods which have very little iron in them. Women generally need a higher level of iron in their diet, especially during menstruation or pregnancy, and should be aware of the possible need for supplementation.

## Calcium

This is essential for healthy teeth and strong bones. Calcium is readily available in dairy foods, but not so common in the purely vegetable diet. Some sources are soya beans in any form, figs, dates and sesame seeds.

## Fibre

This is most important for internal health, especially in relation to the colon or large intestine. Fibre is responsible for lowering cholesterol, reducing constipation, easing haemorrhoids, and lowering the occurrence of heart disease, appendicitis and colon cancer. Research has shown that the food transit time of a person on a typical Western diet of meat and processed low-fibre foods is 65-100 hours, whereas a similar person on a high-fibre vegetable diet has an internal transit time of 20–45 hours. This means that at any given time the person on the low-fibre diet would be holding eight meals of undigested food and waste in the body, while the high-fibre person holds only three. The good news is that as long as you avoid living on processed 'junk' foods, a vegetarian diet is the highest fibre diet of all.

## Carbohydrates

These are made up of sugars, starches and cellulose, and provide us with body heat and energy for physical activities. The point to make here is that some carbohydrates are beneficial to the body from a nutrition point of view, while others such as refined sugars, snack foods, candy bars, etc. provide only calories and no significant nutrients. The best sweeteners to use are those which are the least refined and so retain their nutrient value: for example, blackstrap molasses, pure maple syrup and honey.

## Fats

This may seem an unusual entry in a vegetarian book, however there is a very real tendency for many of us who have taken the step away from meat to compensate with an over reliance on eggs and dairy foods. Butter, cream, eggs and cheese are high in saturated fats and are just as likely to hinder the health, from a cholesterol and obesity point of view, as fatty meats such as bacon and lamb. If you see this situation happening perhaps it is time to look at stepping away from a dependency on animal foods and discovering the benefits of a true vegetarian diet.

# NUTRIENT SOURCES

The idea behind this section is to have a simple reference guide for those who are interested in knowing more about certain nutrients and their sources. For whatever reasons I hope you find this section as interesting as I did when compiling it.

**Protein** (for rebuilding): soya beans and all soya products (e.g. milk, tofu, tempeh, miso), all legumes (e.g. beans, peas, lentils), grains (e.g. wheat, brown rice, oats, barley, millet), nuts seeds, dairy produce and eggs.

**Carbohydrates** (for energy): fruits, vegetables, natural sugars, cereals and nuts.

**Iron** (for the blood): green leafy vegetables, parsley, wheatgrass juice, prunes, most beans, tomato juice, dried fruits, berries, brown rice, broccoli and blackstrap molasses.

**Calcium** (for teeth and bones): blackstrap molasses, dried fruits, bran, legumes, berries, all dairy foods, soya products, tahini, onions, lettuce, cauliflower, almonds, yeast extract, and cabbage.

**Magnesium** (for digestion): wheat and bran, coconut, greens, soya products, nuts, seaweed, citrus fruits, figs.

**Zinc** (for clear breathing): wheat and bran, coconut, greens, soya products, nuts, seaweed, citrus fruits, figs.

**Sodium** (for the intestines): all dairy products, seaweed, eggs, celery, carrots, beets, beans, asparagus, lentils.

**Sulphur** (for brain and nerves): cheeses, cauliflower, stone fruits, peanuts, spinach, leeks, garlic, apples, legumes, horseradish, melons.

**Potassium** (for digestion): potato skin, parsley, cabbage, figs, almonds, yeast, molasses, bran, prunes, bananas, peaches.

**Phosphorus** (for brain and bone): wheat, corn, nuts, yeast, beans, peas, lentils, wheat germ, cheese and milk.

**Silicon** (for nails, hair and skin): most grains, legumes, spinach, lettuce, cabbage, tomatoes, strawberries.

**Iodine** (for glands and nerves): seaweeds, potato skin, garlic, onions, tomatoes, watercress, pineapple.

**Manganese** (for nerves and tissue): almonds, peanuts, pinenuts, mint, parsley, endive, nasturtium leaves, wheat bran.

**Vitamin A** (for growth and well-being): green leafy vegetables, peas, potatoes, celery, squash, yellow fruits and vegetables, avocado, prunes, egg yolks, butter, tomatoes.

**Vitamin B Group** (for good digestion and calm nerves): in general yeast extract, soya products, whole grains, rice polishings and legumes; more specifically:

**Vitamin B1** (thiamine): yeast extract, oranges, wheat germ, peas, soya beans.

**Vitamin B2** (riboflavin): yeast extract, milk, almonds, leafy greens, wholegrains.

**Vitamin B3** (niacin): yeast extract, peanuts, wholegrains.

**Vitamin B6** (pyridoxine): yeast extract, bananas, egg yolks, vegetables.

**Vitamin B12:** spirulina, tempeh, seaweeds, eggs and dairy products.

**Vitamin C** (for general good health): all citrus fruits, rosehips, strawberries, tomatoes, raw fruits and vegetables like carrots and broccoli.

**Vitamin D** (for strong bones): mostly from the sun as vitamin D can be synthesised in the skin with sunlight, also egg yolks, butter, milk and leafy greens.

**Vitamin E** (for reproduction and vitality): leafy greens, vegetable oils, wheat germ, raw fruits.

**Vitamin F** (for strong development): spinach, orange juice, yeast, eggs, nuts.

# HERBS AND SPICES

Herbs and spices are an essential part of gourmet vegetarian cooking. By using herbs and spices subtly one can bring forth a magic that transforms otherwise plain food into a delightful blend of flavours and aromas that make eating an adventure. In the past herbs were not only used for flavouring foods, but were also well-known for their general healing properties and therapeutic value. Herb lore was once a major part of medicinal knowledge, and international spice traders played a key role in world commerce. In more recent times the upsurge of natural therapies and alternative medicine has rekindled interest in herbal lore; for this reason I have included, where possible, some healing properties as well as culinary uses of the herbs in the following chart.

Herbs and spices should be used to enhance the natural flavour of a food, but not to dominate it (though there are exceptions). Usually one or two herbs are sufficient to complement a dish. Spices, however, can be used in combination so as to build a delicate blend of flavours without one in particular dominating. Apart from reading about them, the best way to discover herbs and spices is to use them and find your own ability to create magic in cooking.

Herbs can be purchased fresh at the greengrocer's (usually a limited selection), dried and bottled or packaged at many shops (wide selection available), or grown in a herb garden which can be as extensive as you choose – it can occupy your entire backyard or just a windowbox.

Dried herbs and spices should be stored in airtight containers, preferably in a dark cupboard as the flavours deteriorate when exposed to light and oxygen. The inside of a cupboard door is an ideal place for a spice rack. Naturally fresh herbs are better to use if available, and generally have a sharper, more distinct flavour than dried herbs. In some cases, however, dried herbs will be stronger than they would be fresh, depending on the herb and the conditions under which it has been dried or stored. Spices are best kept in whole form, and ground or crushed when needed with the appropriate implement.

To best access the flavour of herbs and spices, they should be sprinkled into the oil or butter as it heats for the first few minutes, being careful not to let it overheat. This allows the flavour to permeate the oil and then the dish as it cooks.

Herbs used for healing may be applied in various ways. Just using them in your cooking is a convenient form of preventative medicine which is mostly related to aiding digestion and looking after the stomach. For more specific internal application the traditional method is the preparation of a tissane or herbal infusion. This involves pouring boiling water over the leaves, letting this stand until cool, and then straining. As this book is primarily a cookbook, I have restricted the herbs listed on the chart to culinary herbs and some of the more popular herb teas, most of which have healing properties as well as a unique flavour.

The following chart is included merely as a guide to discovering more about herbs and spices. The real knowledge is gained by using them. We hope you have fun finding this to be so.

**Alfalfa Tea** Good for stimulating the kidneys, bowels, appetite and digestion, this tea is highly alkaline and very good for peptic ulcers.

**Alfalfa Seeds and Sprouts** The seeds are rich in silicon, so are good for arthritis and similar pains. The sprouts are full of vitamins and minerals and high in essential amino acids. A highly recommended food source.

**Alfalfamint Tea** Rich in minerals and vitamins, this tea also acts as an antacid, and is good for digestion and relieving gas. It is great for toning up the intestinal tract, and is high in chlorophyll.

**Allspice** This spice is also known as Jamaica pepper and tastes like a blend of clove, cinnamon and nutmeg. It can be used to add flavour to rice, sweet potato, yams, pumpkins, squashes and various soups. It is also very popular in desserts such as steamed puddings, fruit pies and spiced cakes and cookies.

Wild allspice is used as a fever breaker during colds, and as a stimulant for digestion.

**Angelica** The stems of this plant are candied and used for decoration on cakes and desserts and also in jam. The leaves can be used to flavour stewed pears or apples.

The leaves are reputedly good for the skin. As a tea angelica is used to treat bronchial problems, colds, indigestion and colic.

**Aniseed** This gives great flavour to cakes, cookies and pies, bread and bread rolls. It is also good as a curry spice and as a back taste for potatoes and carrots.

Aniseed tea is used as a remedy for diarrhoea, stomach upsets and babies' colic.

**Applemint** see Mint.

**Balm** see Lemon balm.

**Basil** There are two types: bush basil and sweet basil. Sweet basil is the more aromatic and most common. Basil is easy to grow and best used fresh as a complement to tomato, either raw in a salad or cooked into a soup or sauce. It is the main ingredient in pesto sauce and is popular in many other Italian and French dishes such as pizzas, vegetable combinations, egg and cheese dishes. Basil is also delicious with peas and beans.

A member of the mint family, basil is good for relieving stomach flatulence and gas. It is also good for circulation and catarrh problems.

**Bay Leaves** Bay is a herb which combines well with many different flavours. It is great for soups and stocks as well as most vegetables, especially cabbage, aubergine, potatoes and carrots (a leaf in the water while cooking). Bay leaves are also a principal ingredient in bouquet garni. It is best to remove them before serving.

Bay leaves are soothing to the stomach, relieve flatulence, and are also good for the skin.

**Bergamot** The leaves and flowers can be chopped up and used on salads. The leaves are also good in iced drinks.

**Black Pepper** Best used freshly ground as a final touch. As with most spices, ready ground pepper tends to lose its flavour. A word of warning from Dr Bernard Jensen is that black pepper is seventeen times more irritating to the liver than alcohol. He suggests cayenne pepper as an alternative.

**Borage** Both the flowers and the leaves of the borage plant can be used for taste and decoration. The leaves have a distinct cucumber flavour and go well with fruit drinks and wine punch. The flowers are candied and used for cake decoration.

Borage tea is said to dispel depression and is known in Wales as the herb of gladness. It is also used for palpitations, adrenal problems and to increase mothers' milk.

**Bouquet Aromatique** This is a combination of herbs which have been found to complement each other when combined in a tied muslin bag and cooked in with soups, stews and sauces. The herbs used are tarragon, basil, chervil, savory, rosemary and some celery seeds. The bag is removed and the contents discarded after use.

**Bouquet Garni** This is a small bouquet of herbs tied with string and dangled into the cooking pot for soups, sauces, stews and casseroles. The classic bouquet garni is made up of a sprig of fresh or dried thyme, a dried bay leaf and a few sprigs of fresh parsley. The string serves to extract the herbs prior to serving. The choice of herbs can vary according to the dish, however it is best that the number of herbs is kept low so as not to impair their individual flavours.

**Caraway Seeds** Often found in rye bread and seed cakes, caraway seeds are well known for their distinct flavour. They are delicious with cabbage (cooked or raw) and in coleslaw, and are also good in salad dressings, sauces, dips and spreads.

Caraway seeds relieve stomach gas, are good for colic, and are also known as a hair tonic.

**Cardamom Seeds** One of the basic spices used in Indian cooking, and also popular in Scandinavia. They are used in curries and add a nice flavour to rice and sweet potato or yams, as well as being good in cakes, desserts and puddings.

Cardamom seeds are used medicinally for soothing relief to the digestive system.

**Cayenne Pepper** Made from a blend of dried hot chillies, cayenne pepper is used in rice dishes and curries. It also adds colour and a great flavour to vegetables, soups, sauces and salads. I should mention that cayenne pepper is very hot.

Cayenne pepper is a natural stimulant for the body and can be used constantly with no ill effects. It increases the power of all organs and is the ideal substitute for black pepper.

**Celery Seeds** These are good in breads and spreads, dips, sauces, salads and salad dressings, and ground in egg and cheese dishes.

Celery seeds, leaves and stems are good for stomach disorders.

**Chamomile Tea** This is widely known as a tea of many uses. These include calming the nerves, aiding digestion, soothing colic, creating a clear complexion, discharging catarrh, relieving flatulence, and repelling insects when rubbed on the arms and legs. It is a wonderful tonic for all ages. Chamomile plants are even said to be good for the garden.

**Chervil** Characterised by a light aniseed flavour, chervil is best added to food at the last moment. It is a good substitute for parsley as a garnish and is good in salads, soups and dressings or sprinkled on sauces.

Chervil leaves are said to relieve pain when warmed and chopped and used in a poultice.

**Chilli** A cousin of the capsicum, chilli provides the heat for Mexican dishes, curries and other hot foods. Chilli has a great flavour, but due to the heat factor is more popular with some than others. It is best used sparingly at first and then added to taste if necessary, remembering that the heat from chilli can compound throughout the meal.

Chilli is a great internal cleanser. It stimulates the secreting organs and aids in digestion. Learn to love it!

**Chives** Members of the onion family, chives are best used finely chopped in potato salad (or mash), dips and cottage cheese, as a garnish for soups, or sprinkled over finished dishes as a final touch. Chop finely with a knife or use scissors.

**Cinnamon** Actually the bark of a tree from the Laurel family, cinnamon is available in a ground form or in sticks and must be kept dry in an airtight container for maximum aroma. It adds flavour and aroma to fruit pies, especially apple, and can be sprinkled on sweet buns and cakes, as well as coffee and other hot drinks. It is also good in pumpkin and squash dishes.

Cinnamon is a stimulant and has a beneficial effect on the digestive tract.

**Cloves** Created from dried flower buds and quite pungent, cloves are mostly used to add flavour to stewed fruits, especially apples. They are ground for spice cakes, cookies and some sauces, and are also good whole in fruit punch. Depending on the dish, cloves are often better removed before serving.

Cloves have anaesthetic properties and the oil is well known for relieving toothache. They are also good for flatulence.

**Comfrey** Also known as kitbone, comfrey is one of the finest healing herbs known to man. Ironically it has been banned in Australia as a potential carcinogen. (I imagine they're still deciding on tobacco!) Comfrey is not available on the shelf but can be bought as a plant from many herb growers. Young leaves from the comfrey plant can be cooked and served much like spinach, and are very nutritious. The leaves and crushed roots can be used as a poultice to staunch bleeding, relieve sprains and swellings, and heal wounds. Both roots and leaves are used in tea form for internal healing of intestines and haemorrhaging. Comfrey is also used for catarrhal problems, high blood pressure, asthma, bronchitis and colds.

**Coriander** The seeds are used in curry powders, sauces and pickles, while the leaves are chopped and used to flavour or garnish soups, salads, vegetable stews and curries. Coriander is also nice in apple pies and even custard.

**Cumin** The ground seeds are used in curry powders and pickles, and many oriental dishes. Cumin can also be used in desserts such as apple crumble and fruit puddings.

**Curry Powder** This is a mixture of spices originating from India and now popular around the world. Some of the basic ingredients are cardamoms, coriander, cumin, turmeric, red pepper, allspice, cloves, ginger, mustard seeds and nutmeg. There are many different types and mixes which vary the proportions of spices to range from very mild to extremely hot. The best curry powders are chosen through experiment, experience and personal taste.

**Dandelion** Wine, tea and 'coffee' all come from this amazing plant that many call a weed. The leaves can also be used in salads.

As a tea dandelion is a blood purifier and diuretic, especially good for the gall bladder and the liver. It also stimulates bile flow. The milky sap (in summertime only) is also an old remedy for warts.

**Dill** Both the seeds and leaves are used to flavour vinegar and pickles, especially cucumber (dill pickles), as well as soups, sauces and vegetables such as cabbage, zucchini and potato salad. The seeds go well in dips and spreads, and sprinkled over hot buttered vegetables. A sprig of dill makes a good garnish atop a well-poured sauce.

The seeds of dill contain an essential oil with carminative and stimulant properties. Dill water is used by mothers to wind their babies and is good for hiccoughs and as a mild sedative.

**Fennel** The flavour is similar to dill and is used in marinades, soups and sauces. The stalks and seeds are dried and used in Asian-style dishes and some European meals.

Fennel is good for gas problems and colic.

**Fenugreek** The seeds are used in curry powders, pickles and chutneys, and can also be sprouted and used as a nutritious salad vegetable.

Fenugreek tea is good for digestion, ulcers and soothing mucus surfaces. It combines well with comfrey to remove the catarrh from bronchial upsets.

**Flaxseed** High in silicon and vitamin F, flaxseed is good for constipation and bleeding bowel. Also good in tea for stomach ulcers.

**Fo ti tieng** Known in Chinese medicine as the elixir of life, this herb seems to be a most beneficial tonic for strengthening the digestive tract, increasing metabolism and energising the nerve and brain cells. It is found only in certain jungles in the Far Eastern tropics and is said to be the finest of all herbs, tonics and nutrients.

**Garam Masala** This is a mixture of spices popular in Indian cooking. It contains ginger, coriander and cumin amongst other spices.

**Garlic** A member of the onion family, garlic is not really a herb or a spice but is treated as such due to its wide range of culinary and medicinal uses. It has long been the mainstay of much European cooking, especially Italian and French. Use to taste in soups, sauces, spreads, salad dressings, on bread, in panfried potatoes and many other vegetable dishes. Garlic has a great affinity with parsely, which will take away its odour.

As a healer garlic is a folk favourite. It is used to aid digestion, reduce blood pressure, ward off colds, expel catarrh from the chest, and is a powerful antiseptic. It is also most effective in the treatment of worms when taken in capsule form, either orally or as an enema, for a period of three days and then repeated in four weeks.

**Ginger** This is a root which is chopped or powdered and used extensively for flavour in Asian dishes. In itself it incorporates the harmony of opposites known in Eastern philosophy, i.e. it is sweet yet pungent. Try it in stirfried vegetables and other such dishes, as well as in cakes and cookies, puddings and fruit mince.

Ginger is said to be a tonic for the stomach and intestines, and is very good for colic, cramps and relief from gas.

**Ginseng** This is a root which has been used in Chinese medicine for centuries. It is mostly known as a tonic for vitality and a panacea for all diseases.

**Gotu kola** Another Chinese herb known for its rejuvenating qualities and as a food for the brain. Also used by religious groups in India to develop spiritual powers.

**Hing** This is an Indian spice used in place of garlic or onions, which are not an acceptable food for certain Eastern religions.

**Hops** Taken in bitters as a tonic, hops are also used to induce a soothing sleep.

**Horseradish** A member of the mustard family, the root is grated and used raw as a condiment or in a horseradish sauce. Delicious with panfried field mushrooms, baked vegetables, on sandwiches or with tempeh and gluten steaks.

Horseradish is a stimulant for the sinuses and a powerful cleanser of the gall bladder and liver.

**Juniper Berries** The principal flavour in gin. The berries are good in a marinade to flavour tofu, tempeh or large mushrooms.

Juniper berry tea is a stimulant and is good for cleansing the liver and blood. It also cleans the kidneys and soothes urethral infections.

**Lavender Tea** Good for nervous headaches.

**Lemon Balm**The fresh lemon flavour of this herb complements stewed fruits, sauces and marinades. Try a leaf or two in your tea. Also good in fruit punch.

Lemon balm tea is said to cure insomnia, calm the nerves and dispel melancholy.

**Lemon Verbena** Pleasant and refreshing as a tea, lemon verbena is also used in sauces, salads, fruit drinks and compotes.

**Lovage** An uncommon herb, the seeds and leaves of which can be used in soups and sauces, and can be chopped and sprinkled over salads.

As a healer lovage is said to aid digestion and relieve colic. Also good as a diuretic.

**Mace** Actually the outer coating of a nutmeg, mace has a stronger flavour without the bitterness of nutmeg. Great with pumpkin soup, some sauces, desserts, cakes and puddings.

Mace is good for cleansing and detoxifying.

**Marjoram** A similar herb to oregano, the two can be substituted for each other. Most popular in Italian dishes, particularly pizzas, salads, egg and vegetable dishes, as well as soups and sauces.

Marjoram is an antiseptic and cleansing herb which is good for the skin, and relieves headaches.

**Mint** There are many varieties of mint grown but the three most common are applemint, spearmint and peppermint. Mint has many culinary uses. It adds a fresh zing to potato salad, tabouleh, peas, lemon and fruit drinks. Also use as a garnish for desserts and fruit platters.

A great after-dinner tea to freshen the mouth and aid digestion.

**Mustard Seeds** These come in yellow and brown form and are ground to make mustard powder, which may then be made into a paste. This comes in various flavours and styles, and can be used to make delicious sauces and dressings. The whole seeds are good in coleslaw, potato salad and sprinkled on hot buttered vegetables.

As a stimulant for the sinuses mustard is good for relieving croup and coughs.

**Nasturtium Leaves** Chopped and used in salads, nasturtium leaves add a hot peppery flavour. Also great for garnishing dishes or using as an underlay for certain entrees or bread rolls. Something of a memory these days is the nasturtium leaf sandwich.

The juice is said to relieve itching, and is a blood purifier.

**Nettle(stinging nettle)** This is a herb that many would never consider to be edible but is surprisingly tasty and does not sting the mouth when cooked. Rich in minerals, nettle is best picked in spring when it is young and tender. (You'll need gloves and scissors.) Prepare and serve like spinach, or puree into a delicious warming soup.

Nettle tea or soup is a good blood cleanser and clears the complexion.

**Nutmeg** This is actually the kernel of a seed inside an apricot-like fruit. In its shell it keeps well, but when removed must be kept in a dry, airtight container to stop mildew and flavour loss. The ground nut is used in soups and with baked vegetables, especially pumpkin and carrots. Also good in desserts like puddings, pancakes and fruit buns.

Nutmeg is an aid to digestion and helps to calm a nervous stomach. It soothes headaches and is good for insomnia. However, it has a narcotic effect when taken in a large dose.

**Oregano** Slightly stronger in flavour than marjoram, oregano goes well with many Italian dishes such as casseroles, spaghetti sauce, tomato soup, pea soup, herb bread and pizza.

It is said to aid digestion and soothe the stomach.

**Paprika** A sweet, warm-tasting, aromatic red pepper normally used in ground powder form. Sprinkle it into sauces, salad dressings and dips, or use it to add colour and flavour to sour cream for topping soups and baked potatoes.

Paprika is said to stimulate the appetite.

**Parsley** Always best used fresh, parsley is a most popular garnish for many dishes, and has a distinct and pleasant flavour. It can be chopped and sprinkled as a final touch on just about anything, and is a welcome addition to sauces, scrambled eggs and other breakfast dishes. An excellent breath freshener, parsley should always accompany garlic and onion dishes.

As a healer parsley is rich in Vitamin C, iron, manganese and chlorophyll – quite a package. It is a good diuretic and cleans the kidneys and gall bladder. Also good for diabetes and jaundice.

**Poppy Seeds** Delicious sprinkled on bread, cakes and rolls before baking, poppy seeds are also good sprinkled in salads for appearance and taste.

**Rosehip Tea** High in Vitamin C, rosehip tea is also good for the kidneys and bladder.

**Rosemary** If using fresh, either chop finely or use a muslin bag on a string. Rosemary is an aromatic herb most suited to casseroles, soups and many vegetable dishes. Also popular in scones and herb bread, and even fruit drinks and jellies.

Rosemary is said to be very soothing to the brain. A sprig in the bathwater is said to keep you young.

**Saffron** This comes from the dried flower of the saffron plant, and can be used in cakes and buns as well as in boiled rice to give it a yellow colour and light fragrance. Also used in curries.

**Sage** Good in soups, omelettes, cheese and tomato dishes, and vegetable casseroles.

**Savory** Well-known for its use in cooking beans to increase their flavour and make them more digestible by breaking down the enzymes. It is an aromatic herb of the mint family which goes well in salads and soups.

**Sorrel** The taste of sorrel is bitter and lemony. The young leaves can be eaten raw in salads, while the older leaves are better cooked and blended in soups and sauces.

Sorrel tea is said to purify the blood and cure ulcers of the mouth.

**Star anise** This is widely used in Chinese cooking and to flavour rice.

**Tarragon** The leaves are used in Bearnaise, Hollandaise and numerous other sauces, and also in tarragon vinegar. Goes well with tomato soup and in green salads.

The crushed leaves are soothing for eczema.

**Thyme** A popular herb which complements many vegetable dishes including mushrooms, broccoli, beans, lentils and tomato salad and juice.

As a healer thyme aids digestion, and relieves phlegm and mucus, bronchitis and whooping cough.

**Turmeric** This is a yellow powder ground from the turmeric root. It is most commonly used in curries and to colour and flavour white rice. Also adds an exotic touch to simple vegetable dishes, chutneys and pickles.

Turmeric can also be used to relieve bronchial congestion and is good for the gall bladder.

**Valerian Tea** A natural tranquilliser, valerian relaxes nerves and relieves despondency and pessimism. Also soothing for epilepsy.

**Vanilla Pods** Best used crushed to add flavour to custards, desserts, puddings and hot milk. If using bottled vanilla the pure vanilla essence is best.

**White Peppercorns** These are black peppercorns with the outer shell removed. The taste is sharper and the pepper less noticeable if this is needed, for the appearance of a dish. Best used freshly ground.

# GARNISHES

**Sprigs** Best placed on or beside the centrepiece or at a strategic point on the dish to add colour and balance. Use only the freshest of fresh for best results; straight from the garden is ideal. Try basil, thyme, parsley, dill, oregano, mint, celery leaves, watercress, nasturtium leaves, rosemary, dandelion or any other edible flora.

**Sprinkles** This section also covers chopped and ground garnishes and seeds as they are sprinkled too. Best used to garnish soups, sauces, dips, condiments, salads, dobs of butter, sour cream or yoghurt, casseroles and anything that needs a lift in appearance. Use chopped parsley, chives, spring onions, nasturtium and other herbs; ground pepper, nutmeg, cinnamon, paprika, cardamoms and other spices; poppy, caraway, celery, sunflower and other seeds, crushed nuts, herb or vegetable salts, and anything handy that you feel will add the finishing touch.

**Grated Garnishes** Grated garnishes can be fine or coarse, and can even be a single strand to add the necessary touch. Try grated carrot, beetroot, cheese, radish, citrus peel, chocolate or carob (for sweets), and anything grateable that's colourful and tasty.

**Sliced Garnishes** Good for garnishing the side of a dish (nice with a sprinkle) or the edge of a glass. Use slices of cucumber, tomato, citrus fruits, avocado, strawberry, banana, kiwifruit, capsicum, celery, tamarillo, watermelon, rockmelon, pineapple, etc.

**Flowers** Edible flowers are best: these include violets, nasturtiums, rose petals, bergamot, borage, chamomile, jasmine, dandelion and many more. If you are not sure whether a flower is edible or not, use it on the side of the plate for colour and decoration but warn people not to eat it.

**Sprouts** Handy to use as a sprinkle, or for a bed, or just as a fresh and nutritious complement to many dishes as a sideserve.

**Preserves** Another form of garnish to add a little burst of flavour to any dish or dessert you choose. Try olives (many varieties), capers, gherkins, pickled ginger, pickled onions, and pickled chillies; for sweets try angelica or glazed cherries.

**Carved or Cut Garnishes** There are numerous ways to carve or cut fruits and vegetables so they add an exotic touch to your dish. Here are just a few.
- Try cutting celery into 3 inch lengths, then making a series of cuts down the length of the celery from one end to just past half way. Drop them in ice water

and store in the fridge until the cut ends curl back. These make an attractive garnish for salads.

- Cherry tomatoes can be made into flowers by making a shallow incision, with the tip of a sharp paring knife, around the circumference of the tomato (leaving a section uncut at the base), and then doing the same cut at 90 degrees to the first – like dividing a globe into four sections from the poles. Each quarter can then be peeled back towards the base leaving a four-petalled flower with the seeds intact in the centre.
- Cucumber slices can be jazzed up by scoring the skin lengthwise with a fork before slicing.
- Radishes make great flowers if you remove both ends, then make a series of slices from top to bottom around the end of the radish (leaving room at the bottom for it to hold together) and placing it in iced water to open out. You can also buy a device that will make a radish flower with the squeeze of a hand.
- A strawberry fan is made by making a series of parallel cuts down the length of the strawberry, from just below the stem, and then fanning out the sections (like a hand of cards) by applying pressure on the strawberry between the thumb and forefingers.

# RECIPES

## VEGETABLE STOCK

2 LARGE ONIONS

4 STICKS CELERY – TOPS TOO

1 CUP CHOPPED PARSLEY

3 CARROTS

2 POTATOES

3 LITRES WATER

ANY WASHED VEGETABLE PEELINGS

*Dice all vegetables and place in a saucepan with the water. This should be just enough to cover the vegetables. Simmer for 2 hours. Strain stock and simmer liquid for ½ hour. Strain again. You should have about 1 ½ litres of stock.*
*Hot tip: Rock salt can also be added to stock when cooking.*

## CAULIFLOWER AND CHEESE SOUP

2 ONIONS, SLICED

2 POTATOES, PEELED AND SLICED

2 CLOVES CHOPPED GARLIC

1 TEASPOON DILL TIPS

1 TEASPOON CARAWAY SEEDS

1 LITRE VEGETABLE STOCK

1 LARGE CAULIFLOWER

3 CUPS GRATED TASTY CHEESE

300 ml CREAM

1 TABLESPOON SEEDED DIJON MUSTARD (OPTIONAL)

*In a saucepan sauté onion, potato, garlic, dill and caraway seeds. Add stock and ¾ of cauliflower (diced). Cover with water and cook until tender. Break the rest of the cauliflower into florets and in a vegetable steamer, steam until tender. Place soup in the blender. Blend until smooth and strain out lumps. Put back in saucepan, add florets, cheese, cream and mustard. Serve immediately garnished with fresh dill. Serves 6 – 8*
*Hot tip: This soup can be kept for a couple of days in the fridge. Just add the cream and cheese when heating.*

## CREAM OF BROCCOLI SOUP

2 ONIONS, SLICED

2 POTATOES, PEELED

1/2 SACHET DASHI

1 LITRE VEGETABLE STOCK

4 LARGE HEADS BROCCOLI

SOUR CREAM TO TASTE

*In a saucepan sauté onions and potatoes. Add dashi and stock. Cook until potatoes are soft. Add 3 heads of broccoli and cover with water. Cook until broccoli is tender. Be careful not to overcook this soup as the broccoli will lose colour. Blend until smooth, adding sour cream while blending. Then strain to remove lumps. Break the other head of broccoli into florets. Using a vegetable steamer, steam until cooked (do not overcook). Add the broccoli florets to the soup. Serve hot, garnished with a small spoonful of sour cream and fresh dill.*

Serves 6 – 8

Hot tip: *You can add soya milk to this recipe instead of sour cream.*


## CARROT AND CASHEW SOUP

1 LARGE ONION, SLICED

2 LARGE POTATOES, PEELED AND SLICED

1/2 SACHET DASHI

1 LITRE VEGETABLE STOCK

250 g RAW CASHEW PIECES

TAMARI TO TASTE

1 kg CARROTS

*In a saucepan sauté onion, potatoes and dashi. Add vegetable stock, cashews and tamari. Wash and chop carrots, add to stock, cover with water, and simmer for about 1 hour. You may need to add some more water during cooking as the liquid in this soup reduces a lot; just keep carrots covered. Blend soup until smooth, strain to remove lumps. Serve with cream or a spoon of yoghurt. Garnish with parsley.*

Serves 6 – 8

Hot tip: *Walnuts or almonds can be substituted for cashews, though cashews give the best flavour.*

### BEETROOT SOUP

1 LARGE ONION, SLICED

2 POTATOES, PEELED AND SLICED

½ SACHET DASHI

2 BUNCHES BEETROOT

1 LITRE VEGETABLE STOCK

*In a saucepan sauté onion, potatoes and dashi. Add stock and peeled and chopped beetroot. Cover with water. Simmer for ¾ hour or until beetroots are soft. Blend until smooth. Strain. Serve with sour cream and garnish with chopped chives.*

Serves 6 – 8

### POTATO AND LEEK SOUP

2 ONIONS, SLICED

1 TEASPOON THYME

1 TEASPOON BASIL

TAMARI TO TASTE

1 LITRE VEGETABLE STOCK

6 PEELED POTATOES

3 MEDIUM LEEKS

WATER TO COVER

*In a saucepan sauté onions and herbs. Add tamari, potatoes and stock. Slice leeks using the green ends also. In a colander wash thoroughly. Add to soup and cover with water. Cook for ¾ hour or until vegetables are soft. Blend until smooth. Strain. Serve hot with cream or plain.*

Serves 8 – 10

### PUMPKIN AND NUTMEG SOUP

2 ONIONS, SLICED

2 POTATOES, PEELED AND SLICED

1 LITRE VEGETABLE STOCK

½ SACHET DASHI

1 TEASPOON NUTMEG

1 BUTTERNUT PUMPKIN

*In a saucepan sauté onion and potatoes. Pour in stock, add dashi and nutmeg. Peel and chop pumpkin, add to pot. Cover with water. Cook soup for about ¾ hour or until pumpkin is soft. Blend until smooth, strain then serve. You can leave this soup plain or add cream, or serve with a spoonful of yoghurt. Garnish with chives, or a parsley sprig. Freshly grated nutmeg is nice also.* Serves 6 – 8

Hot tip: *This soup can be kept in the fridge for a couple of days. Just heat and serve.*

## SWEET POTATO SOUP

2 ONIONS, SLICED

4 STICKS OF CELERY, SLICED

½ SACHET DASHI

1 LITRE VEGETABLE STOCK

4 SWEET POTATOES, PEELED AND WASHED

*In a saucepan sauté onion and celery in some oil. Add dashi and vegetable stock, then add chopped sweet potato. Cover with water and cook for about 1 hour or until potatoes are soft. Blend until it is smooth. Strain. Serve hot with cream or plain.* Serves 6 – 8

## MUSHROOM SOUP

1 LARGE ONION, SLICED

2 LARGE POTATOES, PEELED AND SLICED

2 PINCHES THYME

1 TEASPOON HATCHO MISO

TAMARI TO TASTE

1 LITRE VEGETABLE STOCK

1 kg SLICED MUSHROOMS

GROUND BLACK PEPPER

*In a saucepan sauté onion, potatoes, thyme and miso. Then add tamari, stock, mushrooms and ground pepper. Cover with water and cook until the potatoes are tender, for about ½ – ¾ hour. When cooked blend soup until smooth. Strain. Serve immediately with sour cream and chives.* Serves 6

Hot tip: *This soup will last for a couple of days in the fridge.*

## TOMATO SOUP

1 ONION, SLICED

2 POTATOES, SLICED

FRESH BASIL AND OREGANO TO TASTE

4 BAY LEAVES

2 CLOVES CRUSHED GARLIC

1 LITRE VEGETABLE STOCK

1 ½ kg RIPE TOMATOES

½ SACHET DASHI

FRESHLY GROUND PEPPER

*In a saucepan sauté onions, potatoes, herbs, bay leaves and garlic. Add vegetable stock, washed and chopped tomatoes, dashi and pepper. Cover with water and cook for ½ hour or until vegetables are tender. Remove bay leaves, and blend until smooth. Strain. Serve with cream, and freshly ground pepper.*
Serves 6 – 8

## SPINACH SOUP

1 LARGE ONION, SLICED

2 LARGE POTATOES, PEELED AND SLICED

1 CLOVE CRUSHED GARLIC

½ TEASPOON NUTMEG

FRESHLY GROUND BLACK PEPPER

1 LITRE VEGETABLE STOCK

TAMARI TO TASTE

1 ½ BUNCH SPINACH

200 ml CREAM

*In a saucepan sauté onion, potatoes, garlic, nutmeg and pepper. Add stock and tamari, cook until potatoes are tender. Then add washed spinach, simmer for 15 minutes or until cooked. Blend until smooth. Add cream and serve immediately.*
Serves 6
Hot tip: *This soup is also nice served with deep fried or panfried tofu cubes.*

## VEGETABLE SOUP

1 ONION, DICED

1 CUP SPLIT PEAS (SOAKED FOR AT LEAST 3 HOURS)

100 g FRESH PEAS

2 STALKS CELERY, SLICED

2 LARGE CARROTS, DICED

2 LARGE POTATOES, DICED

3 BAY LEAVES

1 LITRE VEGETABLE STOCK

FRESHLY GROUND PEPPER

250g SLICED MUSHROOMS

*In a saucepan sauté onion, add peas, celery, carrots, potatoes and bay leaves. Add stock then cover with water and simmer for 1 hour. Add mushrooms and cook another ½ hour. Remove bay leaves before serving. Serve hot with a touch of cream or plain.*

Serves 6 – 8

Hot tip: *Any vegetables that you have around the kitchen can be used.*

## MISO SOUP

1 LARGE ONION, DICED

2 TEASPOONS GRATED GINGER

50 g HATCHO MISO

1 LITRE VEGETABLE STOCK

2 CARROTS, PEELED AND DICED

2 STICKS CELERY, SLICED

2 POTATOES, PEELED AND DICED

¼ CAULIFLOWER

1 STRIP KOMBU

*In a saucepan sauté onion and ginger. Blend miso in with the vegetable stock. To the saucepan add stock and all the vegetables. Break the cauliflower into florets. Add water to cover. Cook until vegetables are tender. Serve immediately.*

Serves 6

Hot tip: *Pumpkin, broccoli, zucchini, squash, snow peas, are also nice added to this soup. In fact just pick your favourite vegetables and make the soup with them.*

## AVOCADO SOUP

4 LARGE RIPE AVOCADOS

1½ LITRES VEGETABLE STOCK

JUICE OF 1 LEMON

300 ml CREAM

NUTMEG

*Blend avocados. In a saucepan heat stock. Stir in avocado and lemon juice. Simmer slowly; do not boil. Stir in cream. Serve hot or cold with sprinkling of nutmeg. This is a very rich soup.*
Serves 6

## BAKED AVOCADO

3 LARGE RIPE AVOCADOS

1 SMALL ONION, DICED

1 LARGE TOMATO, DICED

¼ CUP CHOPPED NATURAL ALMONDS

100 g SLICED MUSHROOMS

1 CLOVE CRUSHED GARLIC

2 TABLESPOONS STROGANOFF SAUCE (SEE PAGE 94)

GRATED CHEESE

*Slice avocados in half. Scoop out flesh and leave shells. Cook onions, tomatoes, almonds, mushrooms and garlic. Add Stroganoff Sauce. Put mixture into avocado shells. Cover mixture with sliced avocado, top with grated cheese. Bake in a moderate oven for 20 minutes or until cheese is golden brown.*
Serves 6

## AUBERGINE PARMESAN

3 MEDIUM EGGPLANTS

2 CLOVES CRUSHED GARLIC

1 ONION, CHOPPED

2 ZUCCHINI, SLICED

100 g SLICED MUSHROOMS

1 TOMATO, DICED

FRESH BASIL AND OREGANO

TOMATO PASTE TO TASTE

FRESHLY GRATED PARMESAN

GRATED TASTY CHEESE

*Slice eggplants in half lengthways. Scoop out flesh with a spoon. Leave shells. Melt butter or oil to grease frypan. Add garlic, onion, zucchini, chopped eggplant flesh, mushrooms, tomato, basil and oregano. Cook until vegetables are tender, not mushy. Remove from heat, stir in tomato paste and parmesan cheese. Place mixture back into shells; top with grated cheese. Place eggplants on trays in the oven and bake at moderate temperature for 15 minutes or until cheese is golden brown. Serve in individual dishes. Garnish with fresh basil or parsley.*
Serves 6

## ASPARAGUS WITH DIJON CHEESE SAUCE (OR WALNUT VINAIGRETTE)

2 BUNCHES FRESH ASPARAGUS

CHEESE SAUCE (SEE PAGE 96)

*OR* WALNUT VINAIGRETTE DRESSING (SEE PAGE 94)

*Cut woody bottoms from asparagus. Steam for approximately 15 minutes. Make ½ Cheese Sauce quantity, adding 2 tablespoons seeded dijon mustard with mayonnaise. Alternatively, use 1 cup of French Vinaigrette Dressing and add 100 g ground walnuts. You can also substitute walnut oil instead of olive oil.*
Serves 4

## GOLD NUGGETS

24 YELLOW BABY SQUASH

1 ONION, FINELY CHOPPED

1 CUP RICE COOKED WITH CINNAMON STICK

⅛ CUP PINENUTS

⅛ CUP CURRANTS

DASH TAMARI

GRATED CHEESE

*Blanch squash for about 3 minutes in boiling water; cool. Fry onion, rice, pinenuts, and currants, add tamari to taste. Slice the top off the squash, scoop out the flesh. (This can be used for soup stock). Fill squash with rice mixture and top with grated cheese. Bake for 20 minutes in a moderate oven or until cheese is golden brown. Serve hot, garnish with tomatoes and watercress.*
Serves 6
Hot tip: *Keep the tops on the squash as they make excellent decoration. Just blanch them for 30 seconds in boiling water to heat.*

## CAULIFLOWER VOL-AU-VENT

1 PKT 60 mm WHOLEMEAL VOL-AU-VENT PASTRY

6 LARGE CAULIFLOWER FLORETS (STEAMED TILL JUST TENDER)

3 GENEROUS PINCHES GROUND ROSEMARY

¾ CUP STROGANOFF SAUCE (SEE PAGE 94)

GRATED CHEDDAR CHEESE

*Warm vol-au-vent pastry in oven. Melt butter or oil in a frypan, add rosemary and chopped cauliflower. Heat and add Stroganoff Sauce. Put vol-au-vent pastry on individual entree plates and pour mixture over pastry. Top with grated cheese. Garnish with fresh rosemary or parsley.*

Serves 6

Hot tip: *Instead of cauliflower and rosemary use:*
- *fresh asparagus with tarragon;*
- *broccoli with basil; or*
- *snow peas with dill.*

## STUFFED TOMATOES

| |
|---|
| CUP RICE |
| STAR ANISE |
| 1 ONION, DICED |
| 2 CLOVES CRUSHED GARLIC |
| 4 SHALLOTS, DICED |
| ½ CUP PINENUTS |
| 1 CUP COOKED CORN |
| TAMARI TO TASTE |
| 6 LARGE FIRM TOMATOES |
| GRATED CHEESE |

*Cook rice — use a herb infuser and add star anise while cooking. Heat a frypan or wok. In the following order, add onion, garlic, shallots, pinenuts, corn, drained rice, and tamari. Sauté until all flavours are mixed. Slice the top off tomatoes and scoop out flesh (this can either be chopped and added to rice mixture or kept for tomato sauce or used for stock). Place some grated cheese in bottom of the tomato shells, then add rice mix. Top with more grated cheese. Bake in a moderate oven for 20 – 30 minutes or until cheese is golden brown.*

Serves 6

Hot tip: *Serve hot garnished with endive or watercress and black olives.*

## ZUCCHINI ROMA

6 MEDIUM ZUCCHINI

1 ONION, DICED

2 CLOVES CRUSHED GARLIC

2 TOMATOES, CHOPPED

FRESH BASIL

GROUND BLACK PEPPER

TAMARI

1 TABLESPOON TOMATO PASTE

2 CUPS CHEESE SAUCE (SEE PAGE 96)

*Blanch zucchini for 5 minutes, cut lengthways and scoop out centre. Leave shells. Chop. Melt butter, sauté onion, garlic, chopped zucchini, tomato, basil and pepper. Cook, add tomato paste and tamari. Spoon mix into zucchini shells. Put into a baking dish. Pour Cheese Sauce over and bake for 10 – 15 minutes or until golden brown. Garnish with a sprinkle of parmesan cheese and chopped parsley.*
Serves 6

## STUFFED MUSHROOMS

5 LARGE BUTTON MUSHROOMS PER PERSON

2 CLOVES CHOPPED GARLIC

3 GENEROUS PINCHES MIXED HERBS

1 SMALL ONION, CHOPPED

2 TABLESPOONS HATCHO MISO BLENDED WITH 500 ml WATER

*Remove mushroom stalks and scrape out mushroom flesh. Keep mushroom shells. Mix flesh with garlic, herbs, onion and miso. Place these ingredients in a saucepan. You may need to add a little more water if miso does not cover the top of mushroom flesh. Cook and reduce until all the liquid is removed. Blend mixture and place back into shells. Top with grated cheese. Bake in moderate oven for 15 – 20 minutes or until cheese has melted and mushrooms are hot.*
Serves 6

Hot tip: *This mix also makes a delicious paté.*

## GRAPEFRUIT COCKTAIL

2 GRAPEFRUIT

½ SMALL PINEAPPLE

½ PUNNET STRAWBERRIES

CHAMPAGNE

*Peel and segment grapefruit; also take the skin off each segment. Dice pineapple and strawberries. Place fruit and champagne in a cocktail glass. Serve chilled, garnished with mint.*
Serves 4


## CASTELLO PEAR

3 LARGE RIPE PEARS

100 g CASTELLO CHEESE

4 TABLESPOONS NATURAL YOGHURT

2 TABLESPOONS CREAM

*Peel and core pears. Slice in half and blanch. Blend cheese, yoghurt and cream until smooth. Serve half a pear whilst still hot in a dish with the sauce around it. Garnish with parsley.*
Serves 6


## BRAZIL CROQUETTES

½ CUP GRATED CARROT

½ CUP RICOTTA CHEESE

½ CUP GROUND BRAZIL NUTS

2 TABLESPOONS TAHINI

¼ CUP CHOPPED CELERY

TAMARI TO TASTE

½ – 1 CUP WHEAT GERM

*Mix all ingredients except for wheat germ. Then add wheat germ slowly until the mixture is thick and you can shape it. Form into croquettes and deep fry until golden brown. Serve with Herb and Yoghurt Dressing (See Page 92) Garnish with alfalfa sprouts, parsley or fresh dill.*
Serves 4
Hot tip: *Cashews or hazelnuts would be delicious in this recipe if you have no brazil nuts.*

## SEAWEED RICE CROQUETTES

1/2 CUP LONG GRAIN BROWN RICE

50 g HIJIKI OR ARAME SEAWEED

2 TABLESPOONS TAMARI

2 BUNCHES CHOPPED CHIVES

1 CUP GRATED CHEDDAR CHEESE

2 EGGS, BEATEN

1 – 2 CUPS WHEAT GERM

*In a saucepan place rice, seaweed and tamari. Cover with water and cook with lid on until rice is cooked. Remove lid to let liquid reduce. Drain to remove any excess liquid. While still hot chop up seaweed into small strands. Add immediately to chopped chives and cheese, stir thoroughly. Add eggs and wheat germ. Combine all ingredients. You may need to add a little more wheat germ. The mixture should be thick so that you can shape it. Form into croquettes and deep fry until golden brown. Serve with Tartare Sauce (See Page 92) and alfalfa, and garnish with parsley.*
Serves 4 – 6
Hot tip: *This recipe will last for a couple of days if kept covered in the fridge.*

## SPRING ROLLS

1/2 MEDIUM CABBAGE, CHOPPED

2 LARGE CARROTS, GRATED

1 PUNNET MUNG BEAN SHOOTS

4 CLOVES CRUSHED GARLIC

1 ONION, CHOPPED FINELY

1/4 CUP TAMARI

1 PKT SPRING ROLL SKINS

*Put all ingredients into a wok, cook until vegetables are slightly crisp. Cook Roll into spring rolls according to instructions on back of packet. Deep fry until golden brown. Serve on a bed of alfalfa sprouts with spicy Peanut Sauce (See Page 95).*
Serves 10
Hot tips: *You can also add shredded tofu to the basic mix. Frozen spring roll skins are available from Chinese or Japanese food shops.*

## GUACOMOLE

2 LARGE RIPE AVOCADOS

JUICE OF 1 LEMON

PINCH CHILLI

1 CLOVE MINCED GARLIC

1 ONION, DICED FINELY

1 TOMATO, DICED FINELY

*Blend avocados, lemon juice, chilli, garlic until smooth. Fold in onion and tomato. Serve with corn chips or vegetable sticks: carrot, celery, zucchini, cauliflower, capsicum or radish.*

Serves 4 – 6

## PEANUT DIP WITH TEMPEH CRISPS

1 CUP ROASTED PEANUTS

1/3 CUP OLIVE OIL

1 CLOVE CRUSHED GARLIC

3/4 CUP WATER

1/3 CUP NATURAL PEANUT BUTTER

2 TABLESPOONS TAMARI

1/2 TABLESPOON CRUSHED CHILLI

2 PACKETS TEMPEH

*Blend roasted peanuts until ground. Add all the other ingredients and blend until smooth. You may need to add a little more water if the dip is too thick.*

**Tempeh Crisps:** *Slice tempeh into thin strips. Deep fry or panfry until golden brown.*

Serves 4 – 6

Hot tip: *You can use vegetable sticks instead of tempeh: e.g. carrot, celery, cauliflower, broccoli etc.*

## CHOUX PASTRY WITH OYSTER MUSHROOM, CORN AND FRESH BASIL FILLING

### PASTRY:

125 g BUTTER

250 ml WATER

125 g WHOLEMEAL FLOUR

4 EGGS BEATEN

### FILLING:

2 POTATOES

1 BUNCH BASIL

TOUCH OF CREAM

GRATED CHEESE

2 CLOVES CRUSHED GARLIC

200 g CHOPPED OYSTER MUSHROOMS

3 COBS CORN, COOKED

DASH OF TAMARI

**PASTRY:** *Put butter and water in a saucepan. Heat till just before boiling point. While on heat stir in sifted flour all at once, stirring vigorously until the mixture is combined and comes away from the side of the saucepan. Remove from heat; add beaten eggs. Beat the paste until shiny and smooth. Remove nozzle from a piping bag. On a greased oven tray pipe 6 – 8 swirls. Alternatively, use a spoon to make moulds of pastry on the tray. Bake in a medium to hot oven for 30 – 40 minutes, until pastry is golden brown and crisp.*

**FILLING:** *Cook potatoes with ¼ bunch of basil leaves. While hot blend with a touch of cream and some grated cheese. Melt butter in a saucepan, add garlic, rest of basil finely chopped (keep 6 – 8 sprigs for garnish), oyster mushrooms and corn niblets. Cook. Then add potato cream mix, and a dash of tamari. To serve slice top off choux pastry. Place some mix in the middle and the rest flowing over the side. Place top back on and garnish with alfalfa sprouts and basil sprigs.*
Serves 6 – 8

Hot tip: *When making choux pastry, a lot of recipes say to start with a hot oven, and gradually reduce the heat. I have found more success in having a constant temperature all the way through.*

**HIJIKI SPAGHETTI**

1 PKT HIJIKI SEAWEED

1/8 CUP TAMARI

2 AVOCADOS

2 CUPS TOMATO SAUCE (SEE PAGE 91)

*Soak seaweed in water for 1/2 hour. Cook in some water, adding 1/8 cup tamari, for 1/2 hour. Halve and slice avocado and place slices on six individual plates. Heat Tomato Sauce, drain seaweed. Place seaweed next to avocado, top with Tomato Sauce. A sprinkle of parmesan is also nice.*

Serves 6

Hot tip: *Any leftover seaweed can be stored in the fridge for a couple of days; it is very nice in salads.*

## VEGETABLE STRUDEL WITH RASPBERRY COULIS

1 ONION, CHOPPED

2 CLOVES CRUSHED GARLIC

4 SMALL ZUCCHINIS

250 g SLICED MUSHROOMS

250 g SNOW PEAS, STRINGS REMOVED

5 TABLESPOONS STROGANOFF SAUCE (SEE PAGE 94)

1 PKT FILO PASTRY

2 PKTS 250 g FROZEN RASPBERRIES

*Panfry onions, garlic, zucchinis and mushrooms. When cooked add snow peas and Stroganoff Sauce. Cooking slightly. Cool. Open filo packet and cut each sheet in half. Melt about 100 g butter. With a pastry brush paint one sheet with melted butter (not too much). Lay two sheets on top, paint with butter and repeat until you have used five sheets. Put a thin line of mixture at one end of the pastry. Roll pastry up folding sides in as you go. Paint butter along the top fold so pastry is totally airtight. Bake in a moderate oven until golden brown (usually 20 – 30 mins). Blend up raspberries. To serve cut each strudel in half and serve with blended raspberry coulis. Serve with salad, garnish with parsley or watercress.*
Serves 10

## VEGETABLE SPAGHETTI WITH PESTO SAUCE

1 VEGETABLE SPAGHETTI

**Pesto Sauce**

½ CUP WALNUTS

3 CLOVES CRUSHED GARLIC

¼ CUP PINENUTS

3 CUPS FRESH BASIL LEAVES

1½ CUPS OLIVE OIL (APPROX.)

FRESHLY GRATED PARMESAN TO TASTE

*Boil vegetable spaghetti whole for 45 minutes. Slice in half across the length of the vegetable so the spaghetti unravels in longer strands. Remove seeds and unravel spaghetti flesh.*
*Place the Pesto Sauce ingredients in a blender, except oil. Blend. Gradually add oil until you have a moist paste. Serve on top of vegetable spaghetti. Garnish with more fresh parmesan and basil.*
Serves 6
Hot tip: *Pesto will last for weeks in a covered container in the fridge.*

## NUT TERRINE

2 STICKS CELERY, SLICED

1 ONION, DICED

2 TABLESPOONS THYME

300 g GROUND CASHEWS

200 g GROUND WALNUTS

100 g NATURAL ALMOND MEAL

200 g COTTAGE CHEESE

2 EGGS, BEATEN

*In a saucepan, fry celery, onion and thyme. Remove from heat and add cashews, walnuts, almond meal. Then add cottage cheese and eggs, mixing well. Grease a 20 cm loaf tin; sprinkle sesame seeds or breadcrumbs to coat the sides of the tin. Add terrine mixture and press into place. Bake for 1 hour in a moderate oven or until golden brown on the top. Serve immediately with either baked or stirfry vegetables and a sauce of your choice: I suggest either French Mustard, Tomato or Horseradish and Dill (see sauces).* Serves 6 – 8

Hot tip: *Other nuts that can be used in this recipe are brazil and hazelnuts.*

## TOFU KEBABS

3 CAKES HARD TOFU, CUBED

50 g HATCHO MISO

2 CLOVES CRUSHED GARLIC

GRATED GINGER

36 BUTTON MUSHROOMS

36 SLICES ZUCCHINI

18 CUBES RED PEPPER

18 SLICES OF BANANA (IN LEMON JUICE)

18 CUBES ONION

4 CUPS PEANUT SAUCE (SEE PAGE 95)

*Blend miso, garlic and ginger with 1 litre of water, marinate tofu cubes in this for ½ hour. Assemble on a bamboo skewer, in this order, Tofu, mushroom, zucchini, pepper, banana, tofu, onion, zucchini, mushroom, tofu. Either deep fry or panfry kebabs until tofu is golden brown. Serve with Peanut Sauce and salad.* Serves 6

Hot tip: *You can use many types of vegetables on the kebabs. Use your imagination and experiment.*

## HERBED QUICHE

### Base:

1 CUP RYE FLOUR

½ CUP SELF-RAISING WHOLEMEAL FLOUR

50 g BUTTER OR MARGARINE

1 TABLESPOON CARAWAY SEEDS

MILK OR SOYA MILK TO MOISTEN

### Filling:

6 SHALLOTS, CHOPPED

¼ CUP CHOPPED PARSLEY

1 TEASPOON FRESH OREGANO, CHOPPED

2 TEASPOONS FRESH BASIL, CHOPPED

4 EGGS, BEATEN

200 g CHEDDAR CHEESE

⅓ CUP MILK

⅓ CUP CREAM

SWEET PAPRIKA

**Base:** *Sift flours in a bowl. Rub in butter and caraway seeds. Moisten flour with milk. Roll out pastry. Press into 20 cm pie dish. Bake in a moderate oven for 30 minutes.*

**Filling:** *Place all ingredients in a bowl and mix well. Pour into pastry case and sprinkle top with sweet paprika. Bake in a moderate oven for 30 minutes or until filling is set.*

Serves 6

Hot tip: *Mushrooms can be substituted for the shallots*

## SPAGHETTI WITH SPINACH SAUCE OR TOMATO AND TEMPEH SAUCE

1 PACKET WHOLEMEAL SPAGHETTI

### SPINACH SAUCE:

1 LARGE BUNCH SPINACH

2 CLOVES CRUSHED GARLIC

½ CUP PINENUTS

2 TABLESPOONS CHOPPED FRESH BASIL

¼ CUP CHOPPED PARSLEY

FRESHLY GROUND BLACK PEPPER

*Wash spinach and remove stalks. Place in a saucepan, cover with water and simmer for 5 minutes. Remove liquid, set aside. Place spinach, garlic, pinenuts, basil, parsley and pepper in a blender. Blend until smooth. You may need to add 1 cup of liquid. Keep the rest as stock for next time you are making soup. Serve spaghetti, pour sauce on top and sprinkle with parmesan cheese if you like.*
Serves 6 – 8

### TEMPEH AND TOMATO SAUCE:

1 LARGE ONION, CHOPPED

1 GREEN PEPPER, CHOPPED

2 CLOVES CRUSHED GARLIC

2 TABLESPOONS CHOPPED FRESH BASIL

1 TABLESPOON CHOPPED FRESH OREGANO

2 TABLESPOONS TOMATO PASTE

1 CUP RED WINE

2 CUPS FINELY CHOPPED TEMPEH

6 LARGE TOMATOES, DICED

BLACK PEPPER

TAMARI TO TASTE

*In a saucepan fry onion, pepper, garlic and herbs. Add tomato paste and red wine. Stir until smooth. Add all other ingredients and simmer for 15 minutes. Combine spaghetti and sauce. Serve with a sprinkle of parmesan.*

## VEGETABLE LASAGNE

2 ONIONS, SLICED

3 LARGE PINCHES BASIL

2 LARGE PINCHES OREGANO

3 CLOVES CRUSHED GARLIC

3 MEDIUM EGGPLANTS, DICED

6 TOMATOES, CHOPPED

4 LARGE ZUCCHINI, SLICED

250 g SLICED MUSHROOMS

6 SMALL TOMATOES

TOMATO PASTE TO TASTE

FRESHLY GRATED PARMESAN

TASTY CHEDDAR CHEESE, GRATED

1 PKT INSTANT SPINACH LASAGNE

*In a large saucepan put onion, all the herbs, and garlic. Cook a little, then add diced eggplant, zucchini, tomato and mushrooms. Cook all ingredients, then add tomato paste to taste. In a baking dish place lasagne along the bottom, a layer of mixture, a good sprinkling of fresh parmesan, and then a layer of cheese. Repeat this again. Cover tray with foil and bake for 1 hour at 180°C/350°F.*

Serves 8

Hot tip: *Any flavour or type of noodles can be used. If you have no noodles, thin layers of tofu or tempeh will do.*

## HERB AND WALNUT BURGERS

1 ONION, DICED

2 TEASPOONS SAGE

2 TEASPOONS THYME

2 CLOVES CRUSHED GARLIC

3 CUPS GROUND WALNUTS

2 CUPS WHOLEMEAL BREADCRUMBS

4 EGGS, BEATEN

MILK OR SOYA MILK TO MOISTEN

*Panfry onion, herbs and garlic for 3 minutes. Remove from heat. Add walnuts, breadcrumbs and mix. Add eggs, then milk if mixture needs moistening. Shape into patties and panfry for 2 minutes on each side. Serve with Miso Gravy or Tomato Sauce (see pages 94 and 91)*

Serves 4 — 6

## MUSHROOM AND ALMOND FETTUCCINE

FETTUCCINE NOODLES, PREFERABLY FLAVOURED ONES
(E.G. TOMATO, POTATO, SPINACH)

2 CLOVES CRUSHED GARLIC

100 g SLITHERED ALMONDS

500 g SLICED MUSHROOMS

1 CUP STROGANOFF SAUCE (SEE PAGE 94)

TAMARI TO TASTE

GRATED CHEESE

*Boil up noodles. Panfry garlic and almonds, add mushrooms. Cook, adding Stroganoff Sauce and tamari to taste. To serve place sauce on top of noodles, sprinkle with grated cheese, and serve with salad.*
Serves 4
Hot tip: Variations: *tomato and basil, tomato and eggplant, or snow pea and mushroom.*

## SAL'S VEGAN MUSHROOMS

8 – 12 LARGE FIELD MUSHROOMS

2 RIPE AVOCADOS, DICED

JUICE OF ½ LEMON

1 PKT TEMPEH BURGERS, DICED

100 g SNOW PEAS, CHOPPED

1 SMALL ONION, DICED

2 TOMATOES, DICED

TAMARI AND TOMATO PASTE TO TASTE

**Topping:**

⅓ CUP WHOLEMEAL BREADCRUMBS

2 TABLESPOONS CHOPPED PARSLEY

1 TABLESPOON CHOPPED DILL

*Scrape flesh out of mushrooms; save shells. In a bowl mix avocados (with lemon juice), tempeh burgers and snow peas. In a skillet fry onion and tomatoes in oil until soft, add tamari and tomato paste to taste. Mix all ingredients together and place in mushroom shells. Top with breadcrumb mixture and bake for 20 – 30 minutes in a moderate oven. Serve with salad.*
Serves 4

## FILLET OF TEMPEH WITH PINK PEPPERCORN SAUCE

2 CLOVES GARLIC CRUSHED

BUTTER OR OIL

2 PKTS TEMPEH BURGERS OR TEMPEH

1 QUANTITY PINK PEPPERCORN SAUCE (SEE PAGE 93)

*Heat oil and garlic, add tempeh burgers (or tempeh with a dash of tamari if you don't use burgers). Panfry about 3 minutes on each side. Heat sauce and serve with salad.*

Serves 4

Hot tip: *Tempeh is also nice served with Tomato Sauce (see page 91)*

## GLUTEN STEAKS

1 TABLESPOON YEAST EXTRACT

1 TABLESPOON TAMARI

1½ CUPS HOT WATER

1½ CUPS COLD WATER

2½ CUPS GLUTEN FLOUR

2 EGGS

¼ CUP MILK

WHOLEMEAL BREADCRUMBS

HORSERADISH AND DILL SAUCE (SEE PAGE 93)

**Stock:**

1 LITRE WATER

1 ONION, DICED

DASH TAMARI

PINCH MIXED HERBS

*Dissolve yeast extract and tamari in hot water, add cold water. Fold in gluten flour. Place on a wet surface. Roll or pat mixture until fairly thin all over. Leave aside. Put all stock ingredients in a pot and boil. Break off pieces of gluten about the size of a thin pattie. Pop them in the broth and simmer for about 30 minutes. Remove, cook and drain steaks. Beat eggs and milk together. To crumb steaks, first coat them with milk mixture then coat with wholemeal breadcrumbs. Heat some oil in a frypan and fry steaks until golden brown on each side. Serve with Horseradish and Dill Sauce.*   Serves 4-6

Hot tip: *It is better to make smaller sized steaks and have two to a serve, as larger steaks tend to break up in the broth.*

## FILLET DE TOFU WITH APRICOT DIJON SAUCE

1 SMALL ONION, CHOPPED

2 CLOVES CRUSHED GARLIC

2 PINCHES DILL

1 TABLESPOON TAMARI

1 DESSERTSPOON DIJON MUSTARD

2 CUPS ORANGE JUICE

1 CUP APRICOT PUREE OR JAM

1 kg TOFU (HARD IS BEST)

CHOPPED SHALLOTS TO GARNISH

*Panfry onion and garlic in oil, gradually add all the other ingredients until you have a smooth sauce. Use a Barmix to blend the sauce if needed. Slice tofu into thin slices, panfry in garlic and add to sauce. Cook on a low heat until sauce reduces by half. Serve with stirfried vegetables, rice or salad. Garnish with dill and chopped shallots.*

Serves 4

## TASTY BARBECUED TOFU

3 CAKES HARD TOFU

**Sauce:**

3 TABLESPOONS TOMATO PASTE

3 TABLESPOONS TAHINI

1/4 CUP TAMARI

4 CUPS WATER

GRATED GINGER

4 CLOVES CRUSHED GARLIC

*Blend all sauce ingredients. Slice or cube tofu (depending on what effect you want). In a large saucepan place tofu and sauce, reduce (see Glossary) for 1/2 hour. If sauce becomes too thick, add more water. The thicker the sauce, the stronger the flavour. This recipe is nice served with fried rice and stirfried vegetables.*

Serves 6

Hot tip: *This sauce can be made up in advance and kept in the fridge in an airtight container for about a week. Honey can be added to taste for a sweeter flavour.*

## VEGETABLE AND LENTIL CURRY

1 ONION, SLICED

½ TABLESPOON BLACK MUSTARD SEEDS

½ TABLESPOON GROUND CUMIN

1 TABLESPOON CHOPPED FRESH CORIANDER

1 TABLESPOON TURMERIC

½ TABLESPOON GARAM MASALA

1½ TABLESPOONS CURRY POWDER

500 ml WATER

150 g COOKED BROWN LENTILS

2 HEADS BROCCOLI

¼ CAULIFLOWER

100 g BEANS OR SNOW PEAS

2 POTATOES, DICED

*Panfry onion in oil, add curry herbs (all at once). Add water and stir until you have a smooth consistency. Simmer for 2 minutes. Add vegetables and lentils, stir and coat with curry liquid. Cook for about 30 minutes, or until vegetables are cooked the way you like them. This curry is nice served with either black rice or brown rice, and with banana slices dipped in lemon juice and rolled in coconut, as well as cucumber and pappadams.*

Serves 4 – 6

Hot tips: *If you like a hot curry add either fresh chilli or crushed chilli to this recipe. If using snow peas add them at the last minute so they retain their crispness.*

## VEGETABLES AU GRATIN

2 LARGE CARROTS

1/4 CAULIFLOWER

1 HEAD BROCCOLI

8 BABY SQUASH

8 BRUSSEL SPROUTS

1 CUP BEAN SPROUTS

TAMARI TO TASTE

1/2 CUP WHEAT GERM

1 CUP GRATED CHEESE

1/4 CUP GROUND BRAZIL NUTS

2 CLOVES CRUSHED GARLIC

2 TABLESPOONS CHOPPED PARSLEY

Cut carrots into rings, cauliflower and broccoli into florets. Slice squash and brussel sprouts. Partly steam all vegetables. Place vegetables into a greased casserole dish with bean sprouts, sprinkle with tamari. Mix wheat germ, cheese, nuts, garlic and parsley together, and sprinkle over vegetables. Bake in a moderate oven until cheese has melted. Serve with salad and herbed potatoes. This recipe can also have one quantity of Cheese Sauce (see page 96) mixed through before baking. You can delete the grated cheese for the topping and add more nuts, parsley and wheat germ.

Serves 4

Hot tip: Any vegetables may be used in this recipe — pick your favourites! Fresh herbs are nice, finely chopped and sprinkled over vegetables before baking.

## CHILLI CON TOFU

1 LARGE ONION, SLICED

2 GREEN PEPPERS, SLICED

5 HOT CHILLI PODS (OR CHILLI TO TASTE)

3 CLOVES CRUSHED GARLIC

3 CAKES HARD TOFU

2 CUPS COOKED RED KIDNEY BEANS

1/4 CUP NATURAL PEANUT BUTTER

1/2 CUP TOMATO PASTE

2 1/2 CUPS WATER

In a saucepan heat oil, sauté onion, peppers, chilli and garlic. Then add cubed tofu and red kidney beans, cook for a couple of minutes. Meanwhile blend peanut butter, tomato paste and water until you have a thick sauce. Pour sauce over tofu and kidney beans. Stir through and simmer on a low heat for about 15 minutes. Serve with a green salad and corn chips.

Serves 6

Hot tip: When cooking kidney beans add a strip of kombu to the water. It will cut the cooking time by half. Tempeh can be used in this recipe instead of tofu.

## SPINACH AND FETTA PANCAKES

**Pancakes:**

1½ CUPS WHOLEMEAL PLAIN FLOUR

2 CUPS MILK OR SOYA MILK

2 EGGS

**Filling:**

1 BUNCH SPINACH

200 g FETTA CHEESE

½ CUP PINENUTS

**Pancakes:** Blend all ingredients. Melt some butter in a medium frypan. Put approx ¼ cup of mixture in frypan. Cook until golden brown on one side, then turn over and cook other side. Remove from pan, add a touch more butter and repeat until you have 10 pancakes. Keep in a warm oven, with greaseproof paper in between them, while you make filling.

**Filling:** Wash and remove stalks from spinach. Boil for a few minutes in a little water. Remove from pot and blend with Fetta cheese until smooth. Fold in pinenuts. Place mix in pancakes, which can either be rolled up or folded in half. Serve with salad and Tarragon Cheese sauce if you like (see page 96). Use basic Cheese Sauce recipe, except add 1 tablespoon tarragon to the butter.

Serves 5

Hot tip: Use your imagination when it comes to the pancake filling — take a look around your fridge for inspiration. Pancakes can be frozen.

## VEGETABLE STROGANOFF

1 LARGE ONION, SLICED

500 g SLICED MUSHROOMS

TAMARI

STEAMED VEGETABLES

½ QUANTITY STROGANOFF SAUCE (SEE PAGE 94)

1 PACKET VEGERONI NOODLES

*Panfry onion and mushrooms in a saucepan, add a good slurp of tamari. Add partly steamed vegetables, e.g. broccoli, cauliflower, carrot, zucchini, snow peas, beans, peppers or whatever your imagination tells you. Stir in Stroganoff Sauce, heat until hot and sauce has coated all vegetables. Serve on a bed of noodles.*
Serves 4-6

Hot tip: *Plain brown rice or fried rice is nice instead of noodles if you wish.*

## SWEET AND SOUR TOFU

¼ CUP LEMON JUICE

¼ CUP TAMARI

1 CUP WATER

¼ CUP TOMATO PASTE

2 TABLESPOONS HONEY

1 TEASPOON MINCED GINGER

4 CLOVES CRUSHED GARLIC

GROUND BLACK PEPPER

2 CAKES HARD TOFU, CUBED

8 SHALLOTS, SLICED

1 RED CAPSICUM, SLICED

500 g SLICED MUSHROOMS

1 CUP TOASTED CASHEWS

250 g HONEY SNAP PEAS, STRUNG

*Combine first eight ingredients and marinate tofu in the mix for a few hours. Heat oil in a wok and add vegetables. Cook for about 3 minutes, add tofu and marinade. Cook for about 15 minutes and add toasted cashews. Serve on a bed of rice, garnished with parsley.*
Serves 4-6

## TEMPEH TEMPTATION

1 ONION, SLICED

3 CLOVES CRUSHED GARLIC

2 TABLESPOONS CHOPPED GINGER

2 PKTS TEMPEH, DICED

200 g SLICED MUSHROOMS

¼ CUP TAMARI

2 CUPS WATER

2 TEASPOONS ARROWROOT

300 g SNOW PEAS

*Heat a little oil in a wok, add onion, garlic, and ginger. Cook for a few minutes, then add tempeh and mushrooms. Add tamari plus ¾ cup of water. Mix arrowroot with rest of water, pour in to thicken mixture. Just before serving add snow peas. This dish is nice served with brown rice or fried rice.*
Serves 4 – 6


## MEXICAN ROLLS

1 ONION

2 CLOVES GARLIC

1 LARGE TOMATO

JUICE OF 1 LEMON

CHILLI TO TASTE

3 RIPE AVOCADOS

1 PKT FILO PASTRY

100 g BUTTER

4 CUPS TOMATO SAUCE (SEE PAGE 91)

*Blend, in the following order, onion, garlic, tomato, lemon juice, chilli, avocado. Open filo pastry packet, cut each sheet in half. Melt butter. With a pastry brush paint one sheet with butter (not too much). Lay another 2 sheets on top, repeat until you have 5 sheets. Put a thin line of mixture at one end of the pastry. Roll pastry up folding the sides in as you go. Paint butter along the top fold so the pastry is totally airtight. Bake in a moderate oven until golden brown, usually 20 – 30 minutes. Serve hot with salad and Tomato Sauce.*
Serves 10

## MAGIC MUSHROOMS

18 LARGE BUTTON MUSHROOMS

2 RIPE AVOCADOS

1 SMALL ONION, FINELY CHOPPED

1 TOMATO, BLANCHED AND SKINNED

1 CLOVE CRUSHED GARLIC

JUICE OF 1 LEMON

GRATED CHEDDAR CHEESE

*Scrape out mushroom flesh. Blend avocados, onion, tomato, garlic and lemon juice until smooth. Fill mushroom shells with avocado mixture, top with grated cheese. Bake on greased oven tray for 20 minutes or until cheese is golden brown.*

Serves 6

## CHOCOLATE AND STRAWBERRY CHEESECAKE

**Base:**

1½ CUPS NATURAL ALMONDS

½ CUP DESICCATED COCONUT

1 CUP ROLLED OATS

⅓ CUP MILK (APPROX.)

**Strawberry Layer:**

1 x 250 g PHILADELPHIA CREAM CHEESE

1 PUNNET SLICED STRAWBERRIES

¼ CUP MAPLE SYRUP

**Chocolate Layer:**

200 g DARK CHOCOLATE

¼ CUP PURE MAPLE SYRUP

200 g PHILADELPHIA CREAM CHESE

**Base:** *Blend first three ingredients, then add milk gradually until pastry is firm. Press into 20cm pie dish and bake for 30 minutes.*

**Strawberry Layer:** *Blend cream cheese and maple syrup together until smooth. Fold in strawberries. Place in the bottom of the cooked pie base.*

**Chocolate Layer:** In a double boiler melt chocolate, add maple syrup and stir. Place chocolate and cream cheese in the blender. Blend until smooth, pour on top of strawberry layer. Cover and chill for at least 2 hours. Decorate with grated chocolate and whole strawberries.

Serves 8

## CHOCOLATE MOUSSE

100 g DARK CHOCOLATE

1 DESSERTSPOON RAW SUGAR

2 EGGS, SEPARATED

2 DESSERTSPOONS CREAM

*In a double boiler place chocolate, sugar, egg yolks and ¼ cup hot water. Beat until smooth. Cool slightly, then add cream. When cold fold into stiffly beaten egg whites. Pour into individual bowls and chill until set. Garnish with grated chocolate and wafers.*

Serves 4

## APRICOT CREAM CHEESECAKE

**Base:**

2 CUPS NATURAL ALMONDS

1 CUP ROLLED OATS

1/3 CUP MILK (APPROX.)

**Filling:**

300 g DRIED APRICOTS

1/4 CUP CREAM

1/2 CUP NATURAL YOGHURT

1 TEASPOON PURE VANILLA ESSENCE

2 x 250 g PHILADELPHIA CREAM CHEESE

1 BUNCH GREEN SEEDLESS GRAPES

1 PUNNET STRAWBERRIES

**Base:** *Almonds and rolled oats, add milk until pastry is firm. Press into 20 cm pie dish. Bake for 30 minutes in a moderate oven.*

**Filling:** *Put apricots in a saucepan, cover with water and cook until soft. Drain and cool. Beat cream, yoghurt and vanilla in a blender, adding cheese slowly. Blend until you have a smooth firm consistency. Fold washed grapes into cheese mixture. Place apricots in the bottom of pie shell, pour over cheese mixture. Let set in the fridge for 2 hours. Top with strawberries and serve. Serves 8*

## BANANA CREAM PIE

**Base:**

2 CUPS NATURAL ALMONDS

1 CUP ROLLED OATS

1/3 CUP MILK (APPROX)

**Filling:**

4 LARGE BANANAS

JUICE OF 1/2 LEMON

2 x 250g PHILADELPHIA CREAM CHEESE

1/4 CUP CREAM

1/4 CUP PURE MAPLE SYRUP

1 TEASPOON PURE VANILLA ESSENCE

STRAWBERRIES AND PASSIONFRUIT FOR DECORATION

**Base:** *Blend almonds and rolled oats, then add milk till pastry is firm. Press into 20cm pie dish and bake 30 minutes.*

**Filling:** *Slice bananas into lemon juice. In a blender put cream, maple syrup, vanilla. While blending gradually add Philadelphia cheese. The cheese mixture should be a smooth, firm consistency. Fold bananas through and place in the cooled pie dish. Leave to set in the fridge for a couple of hours. Top with slices of strawberry and passionfruit pulp.*

Serves 8

## PUMPKIN PIE

### Base:

1 ½ CUPS NATURAL ALMONDS

½ CUP DESICCATED COCONUT

1 CUP ROLLED OATS

⅓ CUP MILK (APPROX.)

### Filling:

3 CUPS COOKED MASHED PUMPKIN

1 TEASPOON CINNAMON

½ TEASPOON NUTMEG

¼ CUP PURE MAPLE SYRUP

3 EGGS

**Base:** *Blend first three ingredients, add milk gradually until pastry is firm. Press into 20 cm pie dish and bake for 30 minutes.*

**Filling:** *Blend all ingredients, pour into pie shell. Bake in a moderate oven for 1 hour or until set. Serve cold with cream or yoghurt.*

Serves 8

## SAGO DELIGHT

**Layer 1:**

1 PKT 250 g FROZEN RASPBERRIES

LIQUEUR (CHERRY BRANDY)

¼ CUP PURE MAPLE SYRUP

1 TABLESPOON ARROWROOT

**Layer 2:**

1 CUP SOAKED SAGO (SOAK FOR 1 HOUR)

JUICE OF 2 LEMONS

¼ CUP MAPLE SYRUP

2 TEASPOONS ROSEWATER

1 CUP SOYA MILK

**Layer 1:** *Defrost raspberries. Heat maple syrup and liqueur. Mix arrowroot with a little water. Pour into maple syrup to thicken the sauce. Add hot sauce to raspberries and chill.*

**Layer 2:** *Mix all the ingredients and cook for about 15 minutes. Cool. Into parfait glasses spoon raspberry mix, to form bottom layer then sago. Top with berry yoghurt and whipped cream.*

Serves 6

Hot tip: *This can quite easily be a vegan dessert by using Soya Custard (see page 95) instead of yoghurt and cream.*


## BLACK FOREST PARFAIT

**Cherry Layer:**

1 CAN PITTED CHERRIES

⅛ CUP CHERRY BRANDY

**Custard Layer:**

¼ CUP PURE MAPLE SYRUP

4 EGG YOLKS

2 CUPS MILK

PURE VANILLA TO TASTE

**Chocolate Mousse:**

See recipe page 77

**Custard Layer:** *Beat maple syrup and egg yolks until pale yellow. Heat milk in a double boiler. When milk is warm add the vanilla maple syrup and egg yolks. Heat and stir until sauce thickens and coats the back of a wooden spoon. Strain and cool.*

**Chocolate Mousse:** *Make one quantity.*

**To assemble:** *In a parfait glass place a layer of cherry mixture, then a layer of custard, followed by the mousse. Top with whipped cream.*

Serves 6

Hot tip: *Any fruit and liqueur can be used for the bottom layer.*

## MAPLE DATE AND WALNUT TART

**Base:**

2 CUPS WALNUTS

1 CUP ROLLED OATS

¼ CUP MILK (APPROX.)

**Filling:**

1 CUP WALNUT PIECES

2 CUPS COOKED DATES

4 EGGS

¾ CUP PURE MAPLE SYRUP

1 TEASPOON GROUND CINNAMON

100g MELTED BUTTER

**Base:** *Blend walnuts and rolled oats, then add milk till pastry is firm. Press into 20 cm pie dish and bake in a medium oven for 30 minutes.*

**Filling:** *Put walnut pieces in bottom of pie dish. Place dates on top of walnuts. Beat the rest of the ingredients until frothy, pour over dates. Bake in a medium oven for approx ¾ hour or until egg mix is cooked.*

Serves 8

Hot tip: *This recipe is the same for pecan pie. All you do is delete dates and substitute pecans wherever walnuts are used. Depending on taste you can add a few more pecans in the filling.*

## ROMANOFF PARFAIT

2 PUNNETS STRAWBERRIES

1/2 CUP KIRSCH

1/2 CUP WATER

1/4 CUP PURE MAPLE SYRUP

1 QUANTITY CHOCOLATE MOUSSE (SEE ABOVE)

WHIPPED CREAM

WAFERS

GRATED CHOCOLATE

*Wash and chop strawberries. In a bowl mix kirsch, water and maple syrup; add strawberries. Chill. Make Chocolate Mousse. Chill. To assemble place strawberries and liqueur in bottom of parfait glass, add Mousse and top with whipped cream. Sprinkle with grated chocolate. Wafers are nice if you have them.*

Serves 6 – 8

Hot tip: *You can use any type of fruit and liqueur for this parfait.*

## RASPBERRY JELLY WITH KIWI AND SOYA SOULIS

**Jelly:**

1/4 CUP PURE MAPLE SYRUP

2 PKTS 250 g FROZEN RASPBERRY

1 CUP APPLE JUICE

1 1/2 TABLESPOONS AGAR-AGAR

**Coulis:**

3 KIWI FRUIT, PEELED AND BLENDED

250 g SOYA CUSTARD (SEE PAGE 95)

**Jelly:** *Place first three ingredients in a saucepan. Heat, stirring all the time and gradually sprinkling in agar-agar. Stir until slightly thickened. Remove from heat and pour into moistened individual jelly moulds. Allow to cool, then place in the fridge until set (usually 1 hour).*

**Coulis:** *In six individual serving bowls place some kiwi fruit puree and some Soya Custard. Use a fork to swirl the colours. Turn jelly out of mould and place in the middle of the coulis.*

Serves 6

Hot tip: *You can use any type of fruit for the jelly; just make sure it is very ripe for best results.*

## COMPOTE OF PORT AND BERRY

½ CUP CURRANTS

250 g FRESH OR FROZEN RASPBERRIES

250 g FRESH OR FROZEN BLACKBERRIES

250 g FRESH STRAWBERRIES

1 CUP PORT

1 CUP WATER

*Place currants in a saucepan, cover with water and cook until tender. Cool. Wash and remove stalks from berries. Mix all the ingredients together and marinate for at least 2 hours. Serve with Soya Custard (see page 95) or cream.*
Serves 4-6

## APRICOT CRUMBLE

### Fruit Layer:

500 g DRIED APRICOTS

50 g NATURAL SULTANAS

2 TEASPOONS CINNAMON

### Crumble Layer

⅛ CUP ALMOND OR OLIVE OIL

⅛ CUP PURE MAPLE SYRUP

1-1½ CUPS SLITHERED ALMONDS

1-1½ CUPS ROLLED OATS

1-1½ CUPS DESICCATED COCONUT

### Soya Custard:

See recipe page 95

**Fruit Layer:** *Place all ingredients in a saucepan, cover with water and simmer about 30 minutes or until fruit is soft.*
**Crumble Layer:** *Whisk oil and maple syrup together. In a bowl place all the other ingredients. Rub oil and maple syrup through until mixture is crumbly. Set aside.*
**Soya Custard:** *Make one quantity.*
*To assemble: In 6-8 individual oven proof bowls or one large one, place apricot mixture. Then a thin layer of Soya Custard. Top with crumble mix. Cook for about 30 minutes in a moderate oven. Serve hot with Soya Custard or cream.*
Serves 6 – 8

## CHOC-ALMOND CREPES

### Crepes:

1 CUP WHOLEMEAL FLOUR

2 EGGS

2 CUPS MILK OR SOY MILK

2 TABLESPOONS CINNAMON

### Filling:

1½ CUPS GROUND ALMONDS

½ CUP COTTAGE CHEESE

⅓-½ CUP CREAM

¼ CUP PURE MAPLE SYRUP

VANILLA TO TASTE

### Chocolate Sauce:

500 g DARK CHOCOLATE

HOT WATER

### Strawberry Coulis:

2 PUNNETS STRAWBERRIES

OR 2 PKTS FROZEN STRAWBERRIES, BLENDED

**Crepes:** *Blend all the ingredients until smooth. Heat a medium fry pan, grease slightly. Pour in about ¼ cup of batter for each crepe. Cook until tops are bubbly and appear dry, turn and cook the other side until slightly brown. Stack on top of each other with a layer of absorbent paper in between.*

**Filling:** *Blend all the ingredients until smooth.*

**Chocolate Sauce:** *Melt chocolate in a double boiler. When it starts to melt add about ½ cup of hot water and stir until you have a smooth sauce. Keep warm.*

*To assemble: Place a few spoons of almond filling along the crepe. Roll up until you have a tube filled with the mix. Place crepe on a serving plate. Put a little Strawberry Coulis on either side of the crepe. Spoon warm Chocolate Sauce on top of the crepe. Garnish with fresh strawberries. This is a delicious but rich dessert.*

Serves 10

Hot tip: *You can make the Chocolate Sauce and let it stand at room temperature and heat it when you are ready to serve.*

## APPLE RICE PUDDING

1 CUP RICE

2 TABLESPOONS GROUND CINNAMON

½ CUP SULTANAS

500 g SOYA MILK OR MILK

6 LARGE APPLES

CLOVES

¼ CUP COCONUT

¼ CUP ALMOND SLITHERS

*In a saucepan place rice, cinnamon, sultanas and soya milk. Simmer slowly until rice is cooked (a little overcooked is best). You will have to keep on stirring it as the rice sticks to the bottom of the pan easily. You may also need to add some more soya milk, to keep rice moist and creamy. In another saucepan, place cored and quartered apple with a pinch of cloves. Cover with water. Cook until tender and blend. Place rice mix in an oven-proof dish and top with blended apples. Sprinkle with coconut and slithered almonds. Bake in a moderate oven for 20 minutes.*
Serves 6 – 8

## APPLE AND BLACKBERRY STRUDEL

6 COOKING APPLES

1 TEASPOON GROUND CLOVES

½ CUP PURE MAPLE SYRUP

2 PKTS (250 g) FROZEN OR FRESH BLACKBERRIES

200 g ALMOND MEAL

1 PKT FILO PASTRY

*Core and slice apples. Cook, by covering with water and adding cloves, till soft but not mushy. Pour maple syrup over blackberries. When apples are cooked, drain. Mix with blackberries and almond meal. Melt some butter. Cut filo pastry sheets in half. With a pastry brush paint a sheet with butter. Place another 2 sheets on top and repeat until you have buttered sheets. Place a couple of spoons of mix across one corner. Roll up pastry, tucking the ends in as you go. Brush some butter on the ends and top to seal it. Repeat this to make the other 9 strudels. Bake on a greased tray in a medium oven for 10 – 20 minutes or until golden brown. Serve with cream, Soya Custard (see page 95) or ice-cream.*
Serves 10

Hot tip: *Cherry brandy is nice added to this strudel.*

## PRUNE AND WALNUT MOUSSE

500 g PITTED PRUNES

¾ CUP NATURAL YOGHURT

1 CUP FINELY CHOPPED WALNUTS

¼ CUP PURE MAPLE SYRUP

600 ml CREAM

*Put prunes in a saucepan, cover with water and cook until tender. Cool. Blend prunes, yoghurt, maple syrup and ½ cup of walnuts. Whip cream with a dash of pure vanilla essence. Fold cream into prune mixture. Put into individual serving bowls. Chill. Sprinkle with the rest of the chopped walnuts and serve.*
Serves 8

## AVOCADO CRÈME CARAMEL

2 VERY RIPE AVOCADOS

3 EGGS

2 EGG YOLKS

½ CUP PURE MAPLE SYRUP

VANILLA TO TASTE

2 CUPS MILK OR SOY MILK

1 CUP WATER
½ CUP SUGAR

**OR**
¾ CUP PURE MAPLE SYRUP
¼ CUP WATER

*Blend avocados, eggs, maple syrup and vanilla. Heat milk to just before boiling point. Stir in avocado mixture. Heat sugar and water, stirring until dissolved. Then boil slowly until thick and caramelly. Alternatively, if using maple syrup, don't heat — just mix with water. Lightly grease crème caramel dishes, put syrup in bottom of dishes. Add avocado mix to fill each dish. Place in a water bath and cook for ½ hour in a medium oven or until set. Chill before serving. This can be made into one large crème caramel, but make sure you have a reasonably shallow tin, e.g. a cake tin. Garnish with tropical fruits that are in season, e.g. strawberries, kiwi fruit, mango and pawpaw. This is a very light, sweet and rich dessert. Try it — you'll be amazed.* Serves 10

Hot tip: *This is a basic crème caramel recipe; you can substitute any fruit for avocado.*

## BAKED APPLES

⅓ CUP CHOPPED PITTED DATES

⅓ CUP SULTANAS

⅓ CUP CHOPPED FIGS

1 TEASPOON CINNAMON

6 LARGE APPLES

2 CUPS APPLE JUICE

1 TEASPOON GROUND CLOVES

*In a saucepan place dates, sultanas, figs and cinnamon; cover with water and boil until the fruit has absorbed the water. Core apples and place four equal slits along the top of the apple. Put the apples in a baking tray or dish with juice in the bottom. Stuff dried fruit mix into the middle of apples. Dust with ground cloves. Bake in a covered dish in a moderate oven for 40 – 50 minutes or until apples are soft. Serve hot with Soya Custard or pouring cream.*

Serves 6

Hot tip: *Any type of dried fruit and chopped nuts are good for the apple stuffing.*

## LAMBRUSCA PEARS

¼ CUP PURE MAPLE SYRUP

3 CUPS LAMBRUSCA WINE

2 CINNAMON STICKS

1 CUP WATER

6 LARGE RIPE PEARS

2 TABLESPOONS ARROWROOT

*Place maple syrup, wine, cinnamon and water in a saucepan. Simmer for 1 minute. Peel pears, leaving the stalks on. Place in saucepan, cover and simmer for 30 minutes. You will need to turn the pears and spoon syrup over them, while they are simmering. Remove pears and cinnamon stick. Add arrowroot to a little water, mix. Stir into syrup and simmer for 1 minute until clear. Pour syrup over pears; chill. Serve with whipped cream or Soya Custard.*

Serves 6

### TOFU ICE-CREAM

2 TABLESPOONS RAW SUGAR

1 x 30 g SILKEN TOFU

½ CUP SOYA MILK

500 g STRAWBERRIES

OR ANY OTHER FRUIT OR FLAVOURING YOU LIKE

*Place all the ingredients in a blender; blend until smooth. If you have an ice-cream machine, pour the liquid in and it will take about 30 minutes to freeze. If you don't, place the mixture in a flat tray in the freezer. When partly frozen, take out and beat until the ice crystals break up. Do this twice, then leave it to set, and you have beautiful ice-cream.*

Makes 1 litre.

### DAIRY ICE-CREAM

#### Vanilla Ice-Cream

2 TABLESPOONS RAW SUGAR

1 TABLESPOON PURE VANILLA ESSENCE

2 TABLESPOONS PLAIN YOGHURT

600 ml CREAM

*In a blender place sugar, vanilla and yoghurt. Blend for about 3 minutes. Add cream and blend for 30 seconds. If you have an ice-cream machine, pour the liquid in and it will take about 20 minutes to freeze. If you don't, place the mix in a flat tray in the freezer. When partly frozen, take out and beat up. Do this twice, then leave it to set, and you have a very nice ice-cream.*

Makes ½ litre

#### Flavoured Ice-Cream

*You can use any fresh or frozen fruit, liqueur, dried fruits, nuts, chocolate, carob – there are plenty of other alternatives you can create. If using liqueurs and fruits, blend with sugar, vanilla and yoghurt. If you want to, use pieces of nuts or fruit; chop and fold into cream mixture before you put it in the freezer tray.*

## MOIST PUMPKIN AND FRUIT CAKE

50 g CURRANTS

50 g DATES, CHOPPED

50 g RAISINS, CHOPPED

100 g APRICOTS, CHOPPED

2 TEASPOONS MIXED SPICE

2 CUPS COOKED BLENDED PUMPKIN

1½ CUPS WHOLEMEAL PLAIN FLOUR

2 EGGS

*In a saucepan put dried fruit and spice, cover with water and cook. Reduce so there is no liquid left. Meanwhile, place pumpkin in a saucepan, cover with water and cook until soft. Blend. Add fruit to pumpkin puree. Stir in flour and beat in eggs. When mixed thoroughly, place in a 20 cm greased cake tin. Bake in a moderate oven for ¾ hour or until cooked. Serve hot with cream or Soya Custard (see page 95).*
Serves 8

## CARROT CAKE

3 CARROTS, COOKED AND BLENDED

1 TEASPOON CINNAMON

½ CUP GROUND WALNUTS

½ CUP CHOPPED RAISINS

2½ CUPS WHOLEMEAL PLAIN FLOUR

½ CUP GRATED CARROT

1 CUP CARROT JUICE

3 EGGS, BEATEN

¼ CUP PLAIN YOGHURT

*In a saucepan place chopped carrots, cover with water and cook until tender. Drain and blend. In a bowl place cinnamon, walnuts, raisins, flour and grated carrot. Mix. Add carrot juice, eggs, yoghurt and carrot puree, slowly. Mix until all ingredients are combined. Put cake mix in a greased 20 cm round cake tin. Cook for ¾ hour in a moderate oven. Serve hot or cold, with cream or yoghurt.*
Serves 8

## TOMATO SAUCE

OLIVE OIL

2 ONIONS, SLICED

1 TABLESPOON CHOPPED GARLIC

½ CUP FRESH BASIL

1 kg RIPE TOMATOES, CHOPPED

1 TABLESPOON TAMARI

2 TABLESPOONS TOMATO PASTE

250 ml WATER

*In a saucepan heat oil. Add onion, garlic and basil, and sauté. Add rest of ingredients and simmer with lid on for 30 minutes. Blend in a food processor. Return to saucepan, heat again and serve.*

Makes 3-4 cups

Hot tip: *Make it a cream sauce by adding ½ cup of cream when you reheat the sauce, or change to chilli sauce by adding ¼ cup chopped hot chilli when cooking.*


## FRENCH MUSTARD SAUCE

50 g BUTTER

1 SMALL ONION, DICED

2 PINCHES MIXED HERBS

DASH TAMARI

2 TABLESPOONS PLAIN WHOLEMEAL FLOUR

2 CUPS MILK OR SOYA MILK

2 TABLESPOONS SEEDED DIJON MUSTARD

2 TABLESPOONS FRENCH MUSTARD

2 TABLESPOONS PLAIN WHOLEMEAL FLOUR

*Melt butter; sauté onion, mixed herbs and tamari. Slowly add flour and milk alternatively, stirring all the time. When you have a nice smooth sauce add mustards, stirring until sauce is heated.*

Makes 4 cups

Hot tip: *If you want a hotter sauce, use English mustard instead of French.*

## WHITE LEMON SAUCE

50 g BUTTER

½ ONION, DICED

2 TABLESPOONS WHOLEMEAL PLAIN FLOUR

1¼ CUPS MILK OR SOYA MILK

2 LARGE LEMONS, JUICED

GROUND BLACK PEPPER

DASH TAMARI

*In a saucepan melt butter, fry onion. Add flour and milk alternatively, stirring all the time. Simmer for 2 minutes. Add lemon juice, pepper and tamari, and stir in. This sauce is very nice served over steamed vegetables, especially cauliflower and broccoli.*
Makes 1½ cups
Hot tip: *1 teaspoon dijon mustard also adds a nice flavour.*

## HERB AND YOGHURT DRESSING

½ CUP NATURAL YOGHURT

3 TABLESPOONS SOYA MAYONNAISE

2 TABLESPOONS TARRAGON VINEGAR

¼ CUP CHOPPED PARSLEY

¼ CUP CHOPPED CHIVES

1 TABLESPOON DILL TIPS

*Place all the ingredients in a bowl and stir until combined smoothly. Serve with Brazil Croquettes (see page 55) or with salad*
Hot tip: *This lasts in the fridge for about 1 week.*

## TARTARE SAUCE

1 CUP MAYONNAISE

2 TABLESPOONS CAPERS, FINELY CHOPPED

¼ CUP CHOPPED GHERKINS

JUICE OF 1 LEMON

3 TABLESPOONS CHOPPED PARSLEY

1 BUNCH CHIVES, CHOPPED

*Combine all the ingredients.*

## PINK PEPPERCORN SAUCE

1 x 85 g BOTTLE PINK PEPPERCORNS

OIL

2 TEASPOONS YEAST EXTRACT

2 TABLESPOONS PLAIN WHOLEMEAL FLOUR

500 ml SOYA MILK

1 TABLESPOON TAHINI

TAMARI TO TASTE

*Put peppercorns and a touch of oil in a saucepan, heat until bubbling. Remove from heat, strain peppercorns from liquid. Put liquid back in saucepan and heat. Stir in yeast extract, then 1 tablespoon flour. Add some soya milk, then add the rest of the flour and stir until you have a smooth paste. Gradually stir in rest of the soya milk. When blended and smooth add tahini, peppercorns and tamari. Heat till slightly thickened.*

Makes 2 cups

Hot tip: *This sauce can be made with cream and milk as well.*


## HORSERADISH AND DILL SAUCE

50 g BUTTER

1 SMALL ONION, DICED

2 TABLESPOONS FRESH CHOPPED DILL

DASH TAMARI

2 TABLESPOONS PLAIN WHOLEMEAL FLOUR

2 CUPS MILK

3 TABLESPOONS HORSERADISH RELISH OR
2 TABLESPOONS, FRESH HORSERADISH

*Melt butter; sauté onion, dill and tamari. Slowly add flour and milk alternatively, stirring all the time. When you have a nice smooth sauce add horseradish; stir until sauce is heated.*

Makes 1 litre

## MISO GRAVY

2 TABLESPOONS HATCHO MISO

300 ml WATER

2 CUPS TOMATO SAUCE (SEE PAGE 91)

*Blend miso and water. Add to Tomato Sauce. Heat and serve.*
Makes 3½ cups

## STROGANOFF SAUCE

3 CUPS SOUR CREAM

1 CUP NATURAL YOGHURT

1½ TABLESPOONS DILL

1½ TABLESPOONS SWEET PAPRIKA

*Blend all the ingredients; add tamari to taste when cooking.*
Makes 4 cups

## VINAIGRETTE DRESSING

½ CUP TARRAGON VINEGAR

1½ CUPS OLIVE OIL

2 TEASPOONS PURE MAPLE SYRUP

2 CLOVES CRUSHED GARLIC (OPTIONAL)

2 TEASPOONS DIJON MUSTARD (OPTIONAL)

*Blend or whisk the first three ingredients together until totally combined. If you like add garlic and Dijon mustard.*
Makes approx. 2 cups

**Variations:**   — **Watercress:** *vinegar, oil, 4 teaspoons maple syrup, 1 bunch watercress (stalks removed).*
    — **French:** *delete garlic from basic recipe.*
    — **Italian:** *delete mustard from basic recipe.*
    — **Walnut:** *use walnut oil, vinegar and maple syrup, plus 200g ground walnuts.*

## PEANUT SAUCE

2 CUPS GROUND ROASTED PEANUTS

1 LITRE WATER

375 ml COCONUT MILK

3 CLOVES CRUSHED GARLIC

1 TABLESPOON CRUSHED CHILLI

1½ CUP NATURAL PEANUT BUTTER

¼ CUP TAMARI

*In a saucepan place peanuts and water. Heat and simmer. Meanwhile in a blender place coconut milk, garlic, chilli, peanut butter and tamari. Blend until smooth. Add to saucepan and stir in with peanuts. Simmer about 10 minutes on a very low heat. This sauce keeps well in the fridge.*
Makes 1½ litres

## CHEESE SAUCE

30 g BUTTER

2 TEASPOONS TAMARI

1 DESSERTSPOON MAYONNAISE

½ TABLESPOON WHOLEMEAL PLAIN FLOUR

1½ CUPS MILK OR SOYA MILK

100 g GRATED TASTY CHEESE

*Melt butter, add tamari and mayonnaise. Stir in flour and milk alternatively until smooth. Add cheese, heat until the cheese has melted and the sauce has thickened.*
Makes 3 cups

## YOGHURT FRUIT SALAD DRESSING

1 CUP NATURAL YOGHURT

2 TEASPOONS PURE MAPLE SYRUP OR HONEY

1/4 TEASPOON NUTMEG

1/4 TEASPOON CINNAMON

1/2 TEASPOON GRATED LEMON RIND

COCONUT OR CHOPPED NUTS

*Mix all the ingredients and chill. Serve on fruit salad garnished with coconut or nuts.*

Hot tip: *You can use silken tofu instead of yoghurt.*

## SOYA CUSTARD

500 ml ENRICHED SOYA MILK

1 TEASPOON PURE VANILLA ESSENCE

2 TABLESPOONS PURE MAPLE SYRUP

2 HEAPED TEASPOONS ARROWROOT, MIXED WITH A
LITTLE WATER

*In a saucepan heat soya milk, vanilla and maple syrup. When warm, add arrowroot and stir constantly until thickened. You can serve Soya Custard hot or cold.*

Makes approx. 2 cups

Hot tip: *Lasts covered in the fridge for 4 – 5 days.*

## SIMPLE SALADS

- Chopped red cabbage with caraway seeds and a touch of Vinaigrette Dressing (see page 94.)
- Grated carrot with poppy seeds.
- Grated beetroot sprinkled with sesame seeds.
- Sliced button mushrooms with Vinaigrette Dressing and fresh chopped basil.
- Cucumber, sliced thinly, combined with natural yoghurt and freshly chopped mint.
- Washed sliced young spinach with pinenuts and Vinaigrette Dressing or lemon juice.
- Cottage cheese and chopped pineapple topped with chives.
- Grapefruit, avocado, lemon juice, chopped mint.
- Tomato and onion, sliced and marinated at least 2 hours in Vinaigrette Dressing and garlic.
- Grated carrots and raisins.
- Lettuce, hard boiled eggs, tomato, parsley and Vinaigrette Dressing.
- Hijiki seaweed cooked in tamari, then cooled and drained, combined with pinenuts or cashews and diced tempeh burgers.
- Diced tomato with fresh chopped basil, which has been marinated in Italian Vinaigrette Dressing for a couple of hours and poured over tomato.

## BROWN RICE SALAD

2 CUPS BROWN RICE

½ CUP CURRANTS

8 SHALLOTS, CHOPPED

1 BUNCH CHOPPED CHIVES

1 CUP COOKED CORN

½ CUP PINENUTS

DASH TAMARI

DASH VINAIGRETTE DRESSING (SEE PAGE 94)

*Place rice in a saucepan, cover with water and cook until tender. Meanwhile place all the other ingredients in a bowl. Drain rice and wash in hot water. Place in bowl and combine all the ingredients.*

*Hot tip: Rice should be added when still hot as you get a better flavour through the salad.*

### POTATO SALAD

1 kg POTATOES

1 BUNCH CHOPPED CHIVES

1 SMALL ONION, DICED

2 TABLESPOONS CHOPPED MINT

2 TABLESPOONS SEEDED DIJON MUSTARD

1/3 CUP MAYONNAISE

*Wash and dice potatoes (don't peel) cover with water and cook. Be careful not to overcook potatoes — they should still be slightly crunchy. In a bowl combine all the ingredients except mayonnaise. Drain potatoes, add to bowl while still hot. Stir and add mayonnaise; leave to cool and store covered in the fridge.*

Hot tip: *This potato salad will last for 4-5 days in the fridge.*

### CITRUS TOMATO SALAD

3 ORANGES

3 GRAPEFRUIT

4 TOMATOES

1/4 CUP VINAIGRETTE DRESSING (SEE PAGE 94)

1 TABLESPOON CHOPPED FRESH BASIL

*Peel and slice oranges and grapefruit into rings. Slice tomatoes. Place alternate layers in a salad bowl. Mix basil with Vinaigrette Dressing. Pour over salad.*

### CORN SALAD

1/4 CUP VINAIGRETTE DRESSING (SEE PAGE 94)

1 TEASPOON GRATED GINGER

DASH TAMARI

8 LARGE COBS CORN

1 CUP SLICED CELERY

1 CUP BEAN SHOOTS

1/2 CAPSICUM, SLICED THINLY

4 SHALLOTS, SLICED

*Mix Vinaigrette Dressing, ginger and tamari. Set aside. Slice corn niblets off the cob. Blanch for 1 minute. Combine with all the other ingredients.*

## ITALIAN SALAD

¼ CUP VINAIGRETTE DRESSING (SEE PAGE 94)

2 CLOVES CRUSHED GARLIC

½ LETTUCE, WASHED AND TORN ROUGHLY

½ CUCUMBER, SLICED

1 PUNNET CHERRY TOMATOES

6 SHALLOTS, SLICED

½ CUP BLACK OLIVES

½ BUNCH WATERCRESS

125 g CASTELLO BLUE CHEESE CUBED

*Mix Vinaigrette Dressing and garlic. Leave aside. Combine all the other ingredients in a salad bowl. (Use watercress sprigs only). Toss all the ingredients. Chill. Pour Vinaigrette Dressing on just before serving.*

## WALDORF SALAD

3 GREEN APPLES

3 RED APPLES

JUICE OF 1 LEMON

¾ CUP MAYONNAISE

3 STICKS CELERY, SLICED

1 CUP CHOPPED WALNUTS

*Core and dice apples, add lemon juice and mayonnaise. Mix well. Add celery and walnuts. Serve on shredded lettuce or in lettuce leaves.*

## GREEK SALAD

1 MEDIUM COS LETTUCE

1/2 CUP BLACK OLIVES

2 TOMATOES, CHOPPED

1 GREEN PEPPER, SLICED

1/4 CUP CHOPPED PARSLEY
OR CORIANDER LEAVES

100 g FETTA CHEESE, CUBED,

VINAIGRETTE DRESSING, (SEE PAGE 94)

*Wash and tear Cos lettuce into pieces. Combine all the ingredients. Toss and chill. Serve with Vinaigrette Dressing and freshly ground black pepper.*


## ORANGE AND ONION SALAD

2 ONIONS, PEELED AND THINLY SLICED

4 LARGE ORANGES, SEEDED, PEELED AND SLICED

5 TABLESPOONS OLIVE OIL

1 TABLESPOON FRESH ORANGE JUICE

1 TABLESPOON FRESH LEMON JUICE

1/4 TEASPOON GRATED GINGER

FRESHLY GROUND PEPPER

*Place onions and oranges in a bowl. Mix all the other ingredients thoroughly. Pour over salad, and garnish with watercress.*


## NOODLE SALAD

2 CLOVES CRUSHED GARLIC

1/4 CUP VINAIGRETTE DRESSING (SEE PAGE 94)

150 g COOKED VEGERONI OR SOYARONI

3 LARGE TOMATOES, DICED

1/2 CUP BLACK OLIVES

2 ZUCCHINI, SLICED

100 g SLICED MUSHROOMS

*Combine garlic and Vinaigrette Dressing: leave to stand 1/2 hour. Combine all the other ingredients, then pour over Vinaigrette and leave to marinate 1 hour before serving. Fresh basil and oregano can also be chopped and stirred through the salad.*

## GREEN AVOCADO SALAD

2 AVOCADOS PEELED AND DICED

JUICE OF 1 LEMON

SHREDDED LETTUCE

1 CUP ALFALFA

1/2 CUCUMBER, WASHED AND CUBED

2 STICKS CELERY, DICED

1/4 BUNCH WATERCRESS

1 CUP HERB AND YOGHURT DRESSING (SEE PAGE 92)

*Place avocado and lemon juice in a bowl. Line another salad bowl with layers of shredded lettuce and alfalfa. Top with alternate layers of avocado, cucumber, and celery. Garnish with watercress sprigs. Serve chilled with a side dish of Herb and Yoghurt Dressing.*


## TABOULEH

1 CUP BURGHUL, SOAKED IN WATER FOR 1 HOUR

2 CUPS CHOPPED PARSLEY

1/4 CUP CHOPPED MINT

1 ONION, FINELY CHOPPED

1 LARGE TOMATO, DICED

1/4 CUP VINAIGRETTE DRESSING (SEE PAGE 94)

2 CLOVES CRUSHED GARLIC

JUICE OF 1 LEMON

*Drain burghul. Mix all the ingredients together except dressing. Mix Vinaigrette Dressing and garlic. Leave aside. Chill salad and mix in Vinaigrette just before serving. Garnish with black olives and parsley sprigs.*

## FRUIT SALAD

2 AVOCADOS

JUICE OF 1 LEMON

¼ ROCKMELON

1 CUP PINEAPPLE CUBES

1 PUNNET STRAWBERRIES

2 KIWI FRUIT, DICED

1 MIGNONETTE LETTUCE

250 g COTTAGE CHEESE

¼ CUP MAYONNAISE

1 TABLESPOON HONEY OR PURE MAPLE SYRUP

¼ CUP CHOPPED WALNUTS

*Peel avocados and cut into strips. Sprinkle with lemon juice. Spoon cottage cheese into lettuce leaves. Mix all the fruit together, then place on top of cottage cheese. Mix mayonnaise, honey and walnuts. Pour over fruit and garnish with avocado. Hot tip: Any type of fruit can be used, so just choose your fruit to suit the mood of your meal. This also makes a nice entrée.*

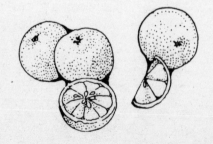

# NATIONAL BANQUETS

The whole idea behind this section is to break the mould. To have fun playing with new styles and themes. I have deliberately written the following recipes with plenty of room for your own input, so what you end up with is your own creation, not ours or anyone else's. Rather than start with precise lists of ingredients all measured to the gram and glossy photos of what the dishes should look like (or else you 'failed'), I would like to suggest that once you've chosen what you would like to create, you picture in your mind's eye just how you'd like it to be, and work towards that. This means that you've got to let go of not knowing what to do, and start putting it together just how you see it in your inner eye. This doesn't mean it's going to work every time, but it's a great way to discover new things about yourself and your cooking. The recipe will give you the basic ingredients and a simple outline of the procedure to follow just to keep the ball rolling, but the finished product depends entirely on how well you create your picture.

As an example, you may love tabouleh with plenty of parsley and tomato in it. So in a recipe with no measurements you can suit yourself as to which ingredients to provide in larger quantities. This also allows you to create the dish according to the number of servings required. If you like black olives then throw a few of them in too. Lash out and surprise people with your own personal touches and innovations. You'll be delighted with the response and before long you will really know that you are an exciting and creative cook.

With the following banquets, try your hand at some innovative international cuisine. The idea is to stick to a theme for the meal, but there is no rule against 'mixing and matching'. The recipes are ideal for dinner parties or group gatherings, and range from complex and exotic to fast and simple. The one thing in common is that they're all delicious!

## LEBANESE BANQUET

**Tabouleh** Soak burghul wheat in warm water until soft (about half an hour). Drain and add finely chopped parsely, mint, onion and diced tomato. Add crushed garlic, lemon juice and olive oil to taste but don't flood it. Sprinkle on sea salt or cayenne pepper and mix well.

*Variations:* use olives, lemon wedges, vine leaves, green pepper, vinegar, cucumber.

**Hummus** (To make a breakfast-bowl full). Start with a cup of chickpeas. Simmer at low boil for at least an hour or pressure-cook for 15 minutes until soft. To puree them you'll need a food processor or an old grinder. Blenders don't normally cope but you can try. At worst a potato masher will do it, but you'll need to remove as many skins as possible. Add a few generous dobs of tahini and heaps of fresh minced garlic. While blending add a pinch of sea salt (optional), some paprika, the juice of two or three lemons and a slurp of olive oil to bring to the right consistency. Water can be added after the first slurp of oil to thin the mix if required. Garnish with a sprinkle of paprika, a sprig of parsley or a dash of olive oil.

### Falafel

Start with ½ kg of cooked chick peas (see above). Grind, wizz or mash them together with a chopped onion, three or four slices of bread with the crusts removed, an egg (optional), a bunch of chopped parsley and a few chopped garlic cloves. While mixing add paprika (or chilli if you like it hot), coriander (fresh is best), and some cumin powder. Leave for an hour if possible to allow flavours to mingle, then roll into patties with wet fingers and deep fry or panfry in oil till brown.

*Variations:* add vegetable salt to bring up flavour, or cayenne pepper; add sesame seeds to the mix or roll the falafel balls in them before frying.

### Vineleaves

These are quite fiddly. You can use fresh vine leaves if they are available. Pick the young tender leaves that have grown to full size. If purchasing the vine leaves (from a health or specialty shop), make sure you buy at least twice the amount needed to allow for flops. Rinse them well in cold running water to remove the brine.

Let's start with the rice mix or dolma filling. First rinse and then boil up ½ cup of long grain brown rice with a cinnamon stick in the water for extra flavour. Remove this when cooked and drain rice in a strainer. Add pinenuts, black currants and a pinch of cayenne pepper. Mix well and allow to cool.

To roll the vine leaf parcels place the leaf veined-side up with the stem towards you. Place a dessertspoonful of the filling on the stem end of the leaf and start to roll the stem away from you. After one revolution fold in the sides and continue to roll up into a tight, neat parcel about the size of a small spring roll. Place the vine leaves in the bottom of a greased saucepan with the flaps down so they stay folded. Stack if necessary but distribute evenly. Cover the vine leaves with a mixture of olive oil, garlic, lemon juice and water and sit a heat-proof plate on top to hold them together while cooking. Bring to the boil and simmer for 20 minutes then drain and cool. Serve at room temperature with lemon wedges and pitta bread.

*Variation:* add onion, chopped mint or dill to the rice mix for different flavours.

### Eggplant Salad
You'll need 4 small eggplants, 2 large tomatoes (chopped), 1 green capsicum (seeded and sliced), 1 small onion (chopped), ¼ cup chopped parsley, olive oil, lemon juice, fresh chopped garlic, and cumin. Prick the eggplants with a fork and bake in a moderate oven until soft (about 30 minutes). When cool, halve and peel and scoop out the seeds. Chop into small strips and add tomatoes, capsicum, onion and chopped parsley. Turn in olive oil, lemon juice, garlic, cumin and mix in well. Serve on a lettuce leaf. Garnish with olives, parsley and tomato wedges.

### Pitta Bread
(Also known as pocket bread)
This can be bought from most shops and supermarkets in plain or wholemeal. Pitta bread can be halved or quartered and used as the base for a Lebanese sandwich using the ingredients above or just eaten on the side with a Lebanese platter.

To add the finishing touch to your Lebanese banquet serve it with olives, pickled chillies, dates, natural yoghurt spinkled with paprika, and plenty of fresh parsley sprigs.

## JAPANESE BANQUET

### Miso Soup
You'll need some hatcho miso, wakame seaweed, hard tofu, a small onion and some finely chopped spring onions. Start by rinsing the seaweed and soaking it for a few minutes in a small amount of water. Chop the onion into small strips and sauté it in a pot with a dash of oil till clear. Puree a spoonful of miso with a little water and add to the onions. Then add enough water for the amount of soup required and stir in the wakame and some small tofu cubes. If large or small amounts of the soup are required adjust the ingredients accordingly, especially

the miso as this determines the saltiness. When hot, serve and garnish with a sprinkle of spring onions. Japanese soup is traditionally served with the rest of the meal and sipped from the bowl throughout.

## Tempura

The ingredients are flour, an egg, tamari, some oil for deep frying and the following prepared vegetables: green and red peppers seeded and sliced into strips lengthwise, string beans sliced lengthwise, mushroom slices, carrot and potato sticks, parsley sprigs and whatever else you might like to try.

Mix the flour and water together. Add a beaten egg and a dash of tamari and blend or mix well to remove all lumps. When the oil is quite hot take a handful of the mixed vegetables and turn them over in the batter a few times to ensure a good cover. When putting the tempura into the hot oil try to keep the pieces separate rather than having them lump together. Deep fry in hot oil for no more than a minute to crisp the batter and lightly cook the vegetables. Drain, garnish with a sprinkle of chives or scallions and serve immediately. A tasty sauce for dipping can be made with tamari, a dob of honey, some grated ginger and a topping of chopped spring onions.

## Tofu Dengaku

Start with a slab of hard tofu, some spinach, hatcho miso, mirin or cooking sherry, shredded ginger root, small bamboo or cane skewers and oil for deep frying. First cook the spinach till soft and blend it into a puree. Heat the mirin with a spoonful of miso and the ginger then stir in the spinach puree. That's the sauce made. Now cut the tofu into bars about the size of your thumb and deep fry them just long enough to crisp the outside (about a minute). Drain, skewer and arrange around a bowl of the spinach and miso dip then serve.

## Sushi Nori Rolls (Nori Maki)

These are delicious and great fun to make, although not always easy at first. You'll need short-grained rice, brown sugar, tamari, vinegar, nori seaweed, pickled lotus roots (not essential), spring onions, carrot and cucumber strips, and a bamboo sushi mat. (Don't let this put you off. Sushi mats are inexpensive and available at any Japanese food store along with the nori seaweed, pickled lotus roots and many other adventurous foods. At worst a cane place mat or even a teatowel would do.)

Let's begin with the sushi rice. You can cook more than is needed here as it will come in handy as an easy side dish. First rinse the rice in a strainer under cold running water as this helps to stop it from going gluggy. Place it in a good sized saucepan and cover with hot water to about 2 inches above the rice. Bring to the boil, reduce heat, cover and let simmer for 20 minutes, being careful not to let it boil dry. The idea is to use up all the water through evaporation and absorption, so that the rice cooks till soft but is not soggy. Let stand to cool. Meanwhile mix some vinegar, tamari and sugar together over low heat to dissolve the sugar. Only a small amount of this mixture is needed so don't go overboard. When the rice and vinegar mix have cooled, place as much rice as you plan to use for the nori rolls in a bowl and leave the rest to be reheated as a side dish. Sprinkle on the vinegar mix and stir it in so as to flavour the rice but not make it slushy. Now you are ready to discover the joys of nori rolling.

Firstly toast a sheet of nori by holding it horizontally over a gas flame or hot plate for a few seconds. Lay out the sushi mat with the slats running from left to right and place the nori squarely on top. Spoon on the rice mix and spread it evenly over the nearest half of the nori sheet about half an inch thick. Make an indentation across the centre of the rice with a chopstick and fill this with a carrot or cucumber strip, a lotus root or two and a spring onion or chive. (There are many variations possible here.) Start rolling at the end closest to you and use the mat to apply even pressure. After one revolution pull the leading edge of the mat away from the rice as you turn to stop it from being rolled in. When the rice has been completely rolled in, and the nori forms a cylinder around the rice mix, give the mat a gentle squeeze and hold for a moment to allow the moisture from the rice to seal the roll. Don't worry if the ends are a mess as they can be trimmed off. If the whole thing is a mess just try again slowly. You'll get it eventually. To prevent the rolls from drying out leave them covered and in one piece until ready to serve. As with most Japanese food, nori rolls are at their best when fresh. With a very sharp knife trim the ends if necessary and slice the rolls in half then each half into three pieces. Garnish with carved radish flowers, wasabi and pickled ginger, and serve with a small dish of tamari for dipping.

## Assorted Accompaniments

Pickled ginger, wasabi (a green coloured root similar in flavour to strong horse-radish, available in dried form which should be mixed with water to make a paste), pickled ginger, rice crackers, umeboshi (pickled plums), grated daikon (Japanese radish), hijiki seaweed, and many other unusual foods from Japanese food stores that I urge you to try in the spirit of adventure.

## MEXICAN BANQUET

Mexican food is great if you want to have everything completed in the kitchen department so that you can sit down with your friends for a delicious and well-balanced meal. It is easy to prepare and most of the ingredients are readily available from your supermarket and greengrocer. The best way to serve a Mexican banquet is to start with the dips as an entree, then lay out the makings for tacos as the main course and let everybody make their own. It's easy and it's a fun way to eat.

### Guacamole Dip
See Sally's recipe on page 57.

### Chilli Con Queso
This is a nice hot chilli and cheese dip. You'll need a bunch of fresh chillies, red for hot, green for mild (if you can't get fresh chillies use the dried ones to taste), some cooking oil, a large onion, cheddar cheese, sour cream and some corn chips for dipping.

Start with the onion, finely chopped, and a slurp of oil in a medium-sized pot. Cook till the onions are soft and add the chopped or dried chillies. Continue to cook and stir for another 5 minutes then add the sour cream and stir till heated through. Remove from heat and let cool for a minute or two, then mix in the grated cheese and leave it to melt. If you are not going to serve straight away then leave the grated cheese until after the rest of the mix has been reheated and add it just before serving. Spoon into a bowl and garnish with a sprinkle of paprika and a sprig of parsley. Serve with hot corn chips.

### Nachos
This is not a dip but can be 'picked at' in a similar fashion. Ingredients are corn chips, chilli powder and grated cheddar cheese.

Place the corn chips in an ovenproof serving dish. Sprinkle evenly with cheese and then with chilli. If you prefer it mild a liberal shake of paprika will do. Place in a hot oven until the cheese melts and serve with the other dips.

### Tacos
These make a great meal and are super easy to prepare. You need to buy taco shells from the supermarket, red kidney beans, an onion, chillies (dried or fresh),

garlic, vegetable oil, tomatoes, cucumber, sprouts, shredded lettuce, grated cheese and a Tabasco sauce.

To make the taco mix you can start by boiling up the kidney beans until soft, or you can cheat and buy a can of them (whichever suits you). Chop up the onion and the garlic and place them in a saucepan with a dash of oil and some chilli. Cook till the onions are clear, then add the kidney beans and some finely chopped tomato. At this stage there are many variations possible, so feel free to create. While cooking the taco mix you should have the shells in the oven on low to freshen them up. Also you can be making up bowls of sprouts, grated cheese, sliced tomato, cucumber and shredded lettuce. When serving place all the bowls in the middle of the table with a basket full of warm taco shells and a bottle of Tabasco sauce, and tuck in.

*Shortcut:* I must say there are some excellent, meat-free chilli sauce mixes available. I have found a jar of this mixed with a tin of vegetarian casserole mince to be a tasty shortcut to an almost instant and hassle-free taco dinner.

## INDIAN BANQUET

Contrary to popular beliefs, Indian food is not always curried and/or hot. It is noted for a wide-ranging use of herbs and spices to create exotic flavours from often fairly bland ingredients. Most Indian cooks specify the use of ghee (clarified butter) for frying, but I find that vegetable oil is much more convenient and quite adequate.

### Dhal

This can be made from split peas, lentils or preferably yellow split mung beans which can be bought at Indian grocery stores. You'll also need tomatoes, some chilli, an onion, garlic, mustard seeds, turmeric, cumin seeds and some vegetable oil.

Firstly add the turmeric, chopped onion, minced garlic and some chilli together in a pot with a dash of oil and sauté till the onions are clear. Then add a cup or two of the beans (or lentils) and cover with water. Add a couple of chopped tomatoes, bring to the boil then reduce the heat and simmer till the beans have dissolved and soaked up all the water. Finally fry up the cumin and mustard seeds in a dash of oil until they start to pop and stir them in to the dhal mixture. Serve hot and garnish with parsley.

### Pakoras

These are vegetables dipped in a tasty batter and deep fried. The ingredients for the batter are a cupful of flour (chickpea flour if available), cumin powder, turmeric, a pinch of cayenne pepper, ground coriander seeds, a dash of salt (optional) and water. The rest of the ingredients are cauliflower pieces, button mushrooms, eggplant cubes and oil for deep frying.

To make the batter mix the flour and spices together with enough water to make a smooth pastey batter. Heat the oil until the batter rises instantly to the surface when dripped in. Dip the vegetable pieces in the batter and place them individually into the hot oil so they remain separate while cooking. When they are golden brown, drain well on absorbent paper and serve hot.

There are many variations possible regarding the choice of vegetables. Some of these could be zucchinis, spinach leaves, banana, potato slices and bamboo shoots.

### Seasoned Rice

This is a tasty accompaniment that could be a meal on its own. You'll need a cup or two of brown rice, some cashews or peanuts, fresh green peas, chopped spring onions, sultanas, garlic, tamari, turmeric and either paprika or cayenne if you prefer it hot.

Wash and drain the rice to remove excess starch. Place in a large pan with the chopped garlic, spices and a dash of oil and stir over medium heat for a minute or two. Add enough water to cover the rice and bring to the boil. Reduce heat, add a dash of tamari and the peas, then cover and simmer for about 20 minutes. When the water has soaked in and the rice is soft, stir in the cashews (or peanuts), sultanas and scallions and serve hot.

### Pappadams

These are a thin wafer-like accompaniment to any Indian dish and can be bought ready-made in many shops or deli's. They are available plain or with flavours such as chilli, garlic and black pepper. To prepare pappadams for serving they must first be fried in oil, which causes them to puff up and become crisp. Fry the pappadam on both sides for only a few seconds, then drain on absorbent paper. Serve immediately or keep hot in oven until needed.

### Cucumber Raita

This is ideal for cooling hot lips and is simple to make. To a cupful of natural yoghurt add some cumin powder, a dash of salt and a sliced cucumber. Stir together, sprinkle with paprika and serve.

## Coconanas

Another easy side dish made up of banana slices dipped in lemon juice and rolled in desiccated coconut.

## Vegetable Curry

If you would like a delicious vegetable curry to go with your Indian banquet see Sal's recipe on page 69.

## CHINESE BANQUET

### Dim Sim

These are a delicious starter and are fun to make. You'll need a slab of hard tofu, an onion, a spinach leaf, garlic, tamari, ginger, oil for deep frying and wanton skins, or spring roll skins cut into quarters.

Finely chop the onion, garlic and ginger and sauté them in a pan with a dash of oil. Slice the spinach leaf up into shreds and add it to the pan, then crumble the tofu in on top. Add a liberal slurp of tamari, then simmer and stir until the spinach is just cooked. Remove from heat, strain and leave to cool. Thaw and separate the wanton skins and place a bowl of water within reach. To make a dim sim, place a spoonful of mix in the middle of a wanton pastry. Lift each corner into the middle, gather and press together with wet fingers. These can be kept in a dish till needed and then deep fried till golden brown before serving. Garnish with alfalfa sprouts and serve with tamari or chilli sauce.

### Spring Rolls

See Sally's recipe on page 56.

### Stirfried Vegetables

The secret of a good stirfry is a hot wok and fresh ingredients. The idea is to cook the vegetables very quickly so as to seal in the flavour and freshness, yet not to burn or overcook. The ingredients are infinitely variable so this recipe is very much a guideline.

You could use mung bean sprouts, sliced bamboo shoots, baby corn, chopped spinach, broccoli, water chestnuts, spring onions and garlic. You'll also need ginger, tamari and a dash of vegetable oil for frying.

Start with a hot wok and add the oil, chopped garlic and some chopped ginger root. Sauté for 30 seconds and add the vegetables in approximate order of their required cooking time (i.e. broccoli takes longer to cook than mung sprouts). Sprinkle with tamari and stirfry the vegetables for up to 5 minutes while turning frequently. Serve piping hot from the wok and enjoy the delicious fresh taste of stirfried vegetables.

If you would like a glaze on your vegetables or would prefer to use no oil, then the dash of oil can be replaced with a spoonful of arrowroot powder mixed into a ¼ cup of water.

### Sweet and Sour Tofu
Another of Sally's delicious treats, on page 72.

### Fried Rice
This is a very popular dish and once again there are many variations. Here is a basic recipe from which you can create your own style.

You'll need some cooked brown rice, minced garlic, chopped spring onions, cooked peas (and corn if you like), eggs (beaten and fried flat like a pancake then chopped into small pieces), a dash of vegetable oil and tamari. Start with the oil and garlic in a frypan. Sauté till golden and add the chopped spring onions and then the rice. Stirfry till heated through then add the peas, corn, egg and tamari to taste. Stirfry another minute or two and it's ready to serve.

### Mushrooms in Blackbean Sauce
This is best cooked in a wok, though a frypan will do. The ingredients are a garlic clove (halved), bamboo shoots (from a Chinese shop), fresh sliced mushrooms, blackbean sauce, chopped spring onions, a slice of fresh ginger root, cornflour or arrowroot, mung bean shoots (optional) and vegetable oil.

Start with the oil in a hot wok. Brown the ginger and garlic pieces till golden, then extract and discard. Stirfry the bamboo shoots for a minute or two, then push to the sides of the wok and stirfry the mushrooms. Mix the arrowroot or cornflour with cold water and add the blackbean sauce. Stir the sauce and the vegetables together and cook until thickened. Serve on a bed of mung sprouts with a sprinkle of chopped spring onions.

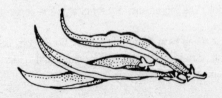

# QUICK SNACKS

This section is mainly for people like us who would like to prepare healthy food for themselves but too often fall victim to the time gobbler. Here are some simple vegetarian snacks which will all pass as meals, allowing you to get on with what you're doing and have that good feeling of something nice in your tummy.

### Avotempeh for two (10 mins)
Halve and deseed an avocado. Slice off a flat spot on the skin side of each half so they sit flat with the seed hole facing up. Chop up some tempeh or tempeh burgers into small cubes and mix with soya mayonnaise, mustard and a dash of vinegar, then spoon into the avocado halves. Can be served on a lettuce leaf with a bed of sprouts. Top off with a squeeze of lemon or a dash of tamari.

### Pitta Pizzas (15 mins)
Set the oven on moderate to high. Start with a pitta bread spread with tomato or paprika paste. Sprinkle with grated cheese and add your favourite toppings: sliced mushrooms, capsicum, pineapple, onion, olives etc. Sprinkle with basil, garlic and chilli if you like, then more grated cheese. Bake on a tray till the cheese is melted and starting to brown. Cut and serve.

### Tacos (15 mins)
See the quick version on page 112.

### Corn on the Cob (6 mins)
A nutritious, delicious and simple snack. The best corn on the cob takes no more than 3 minutes at a simmering boil. Just enough to heat through and serve with all its goodness. It is not true that corn gets softer the longer you boil it. Try corn with a sprinkle of vegetable salt or lemon pepper.

### White Miso Soup (2 mins)
Available at most health food stores. This is as quick as boiling a jug and contains all the goodness of fermented soya beans and seaweed. Ideal for dieting and a delicious snack for between meals.

### Fresh Fruit (0 mins)
Available everywhere, this is Mother Nature's fast food and is too often overlooked for something a little less healthy. Perfect for any snack situation and the ideal travelling food.

### Smoothies (3 mins)

Get a blender and you're in business. Try soya or cow's milk, yoghurt or butter-milk, fruit of your choice, honey or maple syrup, malt, lecithin, vanilla and any-thing else you can find that's nutritious and blend it. Serve in a tall glass with a hydraulic straw, a coffee mug, a paper cup or drink from the jug.

### Soups (10 – 20 mins)

Just like a hot (or cold if you like) vegetable smoothie. Start with a pot, a dash of oil and your favourite herbs or spices. Heat through, then add the vegies gradually – from hardest to softest. I find that soup is the best way to prepare a meal from whatever foods and vegetables you have as leftovers or just those you want to use up. The ingredients are simply whatever is available, so every soup is an original. When the vegies are half-cooked place them in the blender with milk (soy or cow's) and water, and liquefy to the desired level of smoothness. For chunky soup short burst are best. Pour back into the pot and reheat. Add a dash of tamari or vegetable salt. You can cook longer if desired, or serve half-cooked with that extra goodness. Serve with toast and a dob, sprinkle or sprig of some sort.

### Pasta and Anything Goes Sauce (15 mins)

Boil the pasta – spaghetti, fettucini, Soyaroni, Vegeroni or whatever you have – until soft but not mushy (about 10 mins). While this is happening, chop up the vegies you have available and place them, in order of cooking, in a preheated pan with a dash of oil, garlic and basil. Cook through and add tomato or paprika paste, tahini, sour cream or a combination of each (something to sauce it up a little). If the pasta has cooked, it will keep for up to 5 minutes if you turn off the heat and leave it in the boiling water with a lid on. Drain the pasta and arrange it as a bed. Pour the sauce mix into the centre and sprinkle with grated cheese. Garnish with a sprig and serve.

### Welsh Rarebit (10 mins)

Make some toast. Sprinkle on grated cheese, mustard powder, paprika and a dash of vegetable salt and grill until the cheese is melted and starting to brown. Top with a slice or two of tomato and serve.

*Variation:* Tomato or asparagus (or both) on the toast first, then sprinkle cheese etc. and grill.

**Vegetable and Dip Platter (15 mins)**
Make your favourite dip or just use soya mayonnaise or sour cream mixed with a few herbs or spices. Place it in a bowl in the middle of a tray and surround it with raw and lightly steamed vegetable pieces, e.g. beans, snow peas, carrot sticks, cauliflower or broccoli florets, sliced capsicum, button mushrooms etc. A delicious and complete meal in itself.

**Baked Potatoes**
These take time to cook but there is virtually no preparation. Wash the spuds and place them unpeeled in a hot oven for approximately 1 1/2 hours. If you can pierce them through easily with a knife, you know they're cooked inside. Serve with your favourite topping and some sprouts or salad.

**Guacomole (10 mins)**
See Sal's recipe on page 57. Serve with hot corn chips.

**Lettuce Leaf Salad Roll (2 mins)**
Peel off a large lettuce leaf and fill with tomato, sprouts, spring onion, cucumber, perhaps a slab or sprinkle of cheese and a dob of soya mayonnaise or French mustard. Roll up and eat.

**Tempeh Burgers (8 mins)**
These are available at health food stores and are a great source of protein, Vitamin B12 and iron. Serve hot or cold in a roll with assorted salad and condiments.

**Sprouts (0 mins)**
Sprouts are an ideal food to have handy. They are the perfect complement to almost any meal and are a great source of nutrition and living energy. These days they are available in most supermarkets and stores. It is also quite easy and fun to grow your own and have a constant fresh supply. Getting into the habit of adding sprouts to any snack or meal is a great way to ensure a good healthy diet.

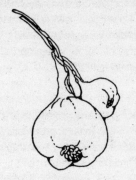

# POT POURRI

This is a collection of information on many things that Sally and I have discovered since we stepped onto the vegetarian path. Some of the tips are actually warnings as to the discreet use of animal by-products in many of the foods that we could eat quite innocently on a vegetarian diet. There are also tips on foods which we have found to be better for us in our diet. We hope you find this section both interesting and helpful in seeing you along your own path.

Did you know that many of the cheeses available today contain rennet, which has been obtained from the inside of a calf's stomach? This is the common practice in cheese-making, even though there are vegetable rennets and microbial rennets available. I would venture to say that this will not change until more people start specifically asking for animal-rennet-free cheeses. At present there are some vegetable rennet cheeses on the market which are well worth knowing about. These are all Norco cheeses, all United Dairies cheeses, Kraft Philadephia, Parmesan and Romano, and some lesser known brands available from your health food shop.

Another sad fact in the dairy industry is the use of gelatine (a thickener made from boiled-down animal hooves, bones and cartilages) in thickened cream. As yet there is no substitute other than plain cream thickened at home with arrowroot or kuzu. Keep an eye out for gelatine in many processed foods.

Pure maple syrup is one of the most natural and least processed sweeteners on the market. It contains essential minerals such as calcium, sodium and potassium and is totally gluten-free.

Free-range eggs are the eggs laid by hens which are kept in an open-range farming system. They are free to scratch around and do what hens do other than just lay eggs. This is in contrast to the much more common (and profitable) practice of battery farming where the chickens are forced to live out their lives in rows upon rows of tiny cages with up to three hens in each cage. These have a sloping wire floor and artificial light. It is common practice for the hens to have half their beak removed or a pair of opaque 'spectacles' fitted to stop them pecking each other to death as a result of the stress. This is a far cry from the image many of us have of the 'farm fresh egg'. While some may argue the quality difference in the egg, I feel from a humane point of view that the choice is clear.

An excellent way to stay healthy, alert and avoid internal upsets when travelling over long distances is to eat fresh fruit, raw salad vegetables and nuts, and avoid the convenience foods so readily available in most transport terminals. This is also a good rule to follow when visiting countries where hygiene and cooking methods are even remotely questionable. Better safe than sick.

Lemon juice is great for removing onion and garlic smells from the hands. Parsley will do the same for the breath.

Scissors are good to use for cutting beans diagonally.

Lemons will give more juice when squeezed if they are placed in hot water for a few minutes beforehand.

A good rule to follow when boiling a vegetable is to consider how it grows. If it grows within the earth (root vegetable) then start it in cold water and cover it with a lid. If it grows above the ground in the sunshine then start it in boiling water and leave the lid off. Don't overboil vegetables. They are ideal when tender yet still crisp.

An alternative to boiling vegetables is steaming them. The advantage is minimal nutrient loss through the leaching effect of the water. You can buy an excellent bamboo steamer at most Chinese shops.

A handy rule to know as a guide to balanced nutrition is the rule of colour. Foods of different colours generally contain different nutrients. If you include at least three different colours each meal and vary the colours when possible then you're on the way to a healthy balanced diet.

To stop rice or pasta from boiling over when cooking, try greasing the top 2 inches of the inside of the pan.

Many biscuits and cookies on the market contain animal fat (lard). We recommend reading the ingredients and if still not sure contacting the manufacturer.

Sally and I are both against the use of microwave ovens. We have never used one in our restaurant and never will despite the obvious time-saving advantages and other conveniences of microwave cooking. We have no proof to show that our decision is correct, but our reasoning is thus.

It is common knowledge that microwaves are harmful to the human body on a physical level, but damage to the far more sensitive etheric (or energy) body is generally not considered. In our daily lives we are subjected to natural forms of microwave radiation from the sun and cosmos which we have lived with and adapted to over thousands of years. The intensity and vibration of the microwaves generated by a microwave oven however, are far stronger and of a different frequency from natural microwave radiation. Microwave ovens work by causing the water molecules in food to vibrate in sympathy (or with the same resonance) and so create heat through friction. The ability of a water molecule to resonate (much like a bell or tuning fork) with this frequency for a significant period of time after exposure to the microwaves is the main reason for us not using this method of heating and avoiding microwaved food in our own diets.

# GLOSSARY

**Agar-Agar**  This is a form of gelatin which is extracted from seaweed. It is rich in vitamins and minerals and sets much faster than animal-derived gelatin.

**Arrowroot Flour**  A starchy flour extracted from a plant root and used as a thickener for sauces, soups and desserts. Also good as a glaze for stirfried vegetables.

**Blanch**  Partly cook in already boiling water. Much like deep frying with water instead of oil.

**Burghul**  Cracked wheat available from most health food and Indian shops.

**Capsicum**  A common word for peppers of all kinds, but mostly used in reference to red and green mild peppers *(Capsicum annum)*.

**Coulis**  French word for blended sauce or puree.

**Dashi**  A stock for soups and sauces which is made from seaweed. Can be purchased in dried form from Japanese and health food shops and comes in two varieties. Be careful to read the packet as one has bonito (dried fish flakes) in it.

**Eggplant**  *(Solanum melongena)* A fleshy vegetable also known as aubergine.

**Filo Pastry**  Very thin sheets of pastry which, when layered and brushed with butter, bake to form a light flaky crust for any number of fillings.

**Hijiki**  A variety of Japanese sea vegetable which is bought in dried form and when soaked forms long black strands. Quite decorative and very tasty when prepared correctly.

**Kombu**  A sea vegetable from Japan. Kombu has great digestive properties and is used when cooking beans or lentils to break down the enzymes and make them easier to digest. Also a versatile vegetable for other uses.

**Legumes**  These are the beans, peas and pulses which make up such a large part of the vegetarian diet. High in protein and many other nutritious goodies.

**Mirin**  A cooking wine made from rice.

**Miso**   A wonderful food from Japan, Miso is made from fermented soya beans, koji (enzymes which aid digestion and assimilation), sea salt and different grains to vary the flavour. There are many varieties of miso and all are nutritious and great for enhancing flavour. When miso is mentioned in this book we are referring to the thick, dark brown miso called hatcho miso. Other varieties include natto miso (with barley, kombu and ginger), soba miso (with buckwheat), mugi miso (with barley), genmai miso (with brown rice) and kome miso (with white rice).

**Muslin Bag**   Muslin is a fine, thin cotton fabric made in India. The muslin bag is used in cooking to allow the flavour of herbs to permeate a dish while cooking and then be easily removed before serving.

**Nori**   Another Japanese sea vegetable which is processed into thin paperlike sheets and used to wrap rice as in nori rolls, or sliced and used as a garnish.

**Pulse**   See legumes.

**Puree**   To turn food into a pulpy liquid by blending in a food processor or forcing through a sieve.

**Sauté**   To quickfry in a pan with oil or butter.

**Scallion**   *(Allium ascalonicum)* Another name for spring onion or shallot.

**Spaghetti Vegetable**   A variety of the vegetable marrow *(Cucurbita pepo ovifera)* which is full of spaghetti-like strands.

**Sprouts**   The small sprouted seedlings of certain edible grains containing good nutrition and living energy.

**Reduce**   This is a method by which food is concentrated and flavour intensified by evaporating the moisture from the dish over high heat.

**Rosewater**   A flavouring agent used to enhance desserts, cakes, and confectionery. Use in similar fashion to vanilla essence.

**Shoyu**   See tamari.

**Soyaroni**   Brand name for a type of pasta made from soya beans.

**Tahini**   A paste or spread similar to smooth peanut butter which is made from ground sesame seeds. Originated in the Middle East.

**Tamari**   A naturally fermented soya sauce from Japan which can be bought in a number of varieties including natural, low-salt and gluten-free (also known as shoyu).

**Tempeh**   Pronounced 'tempay'. This is another soya product, made from whole soya beans which have been fermented in a rhyzopus culture. This breaks down certain enzymes to make tempeh a very rich sauce of protein and B vitamins (especially the controversial B12).

**Tempeh Burgers**   Brand name for a pattie or burger made from tempeh, lemon juice, cider vinegar, shoyu and spices.

**Tissane**   Old word for infusion or herbal tea used for medicinal purposes.

**Tofu**   This is the traditional name for soya bean curd. It is made by straining the curdled soy milk and pressing to remove moisture. An ideal food, tofu is high in protein and minerals, low in fat, and readily takes on various flavours for versatile cooking. Tofu is available in varying consistencies from hard to silken, depending on the water content.

**Vegeroni**   Brand name for a type of pasta made from vegetables.

**Zucchini**   A vegetable from the marrow family, also known as courgette. It is a small variety of the vegetable marrow. *(Cucurbita pepo ovifera)*.

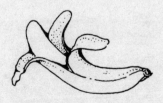

# BIBLIOGRAPHY

Cox, M., and Crockett, D., *The New Vegetarian*, Wellingborough 1985, Thorsons
Hare Krishna Movement, *The Higher Taste*, New York 1983, Iskcon/Bhaktivedanta Book Trust
Harrop, R., (ed.), *Encyclopedia of Herbs*, London 1985, Marshall Cavendish
Hemphill, J., and R., *Hemphill's Herbs for Health*, Sydney 1986, Lansdowne Press
James, I., *Vegetarian Cuisine*, Wellingborough 1976, Thorsons/Vegetarian Society
Jensen, B., *Nature Has a Remedy*, Escondido 1979, self-published
Lappe, F.M., *Diet for a Small Planet*, New York 1983, Ballantine
Lewis, L., *Vegetarian Dinner Parties*, Wellingborough 1983, Thorsons
Parnham, B., *What's Wrong With Eating Meat?*, Denver 1979, Ananda Marga Publications
Phillips, D.A., *New Dimensions Recipe Book*, Sydney 1984, Angus & Robertson
Raja Yoga Centre, *Eating for Immortality*, Sydney 1983, Serge Martich — Osterman
Southey, P., *Gourmet Cooking Without Meat*, London 1980, Marshall Cavendish
Weber, M., *The Australian and New Zealand Book of Whole Meals*, Sydney 1983, Doubleday
Wigmore, A., *Spiritual — Physical Survival Thru Sprouting*, Boston n.d., Hippocrates Health Institute

*Note:* We gained information and assistance from many great people's books while writing this book, and to these people we'd like to say thank you for sharing your knowledge, so that it could be shared again and again by others.

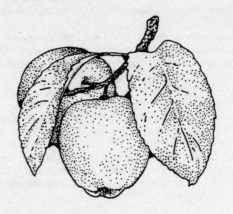

# GREAT QUOTES

● 'It is my view that the vegetarian manner of living, by its purely physical effect on the human temperament, would most beneficially influence the lot of mankind.'
*Albert Einstein*

● 'Animals are my friends . . . and I don't eat my friends.'
*George Bernard Shaw*

● 'O my fellow men, do not defile your bodies with sinful foods . . . The earth affords a lavish supply of riches, of innocent foods, and offers you banquets that involve no bloodshed or slaughter.'
*Pythagoras*

● 'He who does not value life does not deserve it.'
*Leonardo da Vinci*

● ' . . . man supresses in himself, unnecessarily, the highest spiritual capacity — that of sympathy and pity towards living creatures like himself — and by violating his own feelings becomes cruel.'
*Leo Tolstoy*

● 'Truly man is the king of beasts, for his brutality exceeds them. We live by the death of others. We are burial places! I have since an early age abjured the use of meat, and the time will come when men will look upon the murder of animals as they now look upon the murder of men.'
*Leonardo da Vinci*

● 'He that killeth an ox is as if he slew a man.'
*The Holy Bible, King James Version, Isaiah 66:3*

● 'World peace, or any other kind of peace, depends greatly on the attitude of the mind. Vegetarianism can bring about the right mental attitude for peace . . . it holds forth a better way of life, which, if practised universally, can lead to a better, more just and more peaceful community of nations.'
*U Nu (former Prime Minister of Burma)*

● 'I have no doubt that it is part of the destiny of the human race, in its gradual improvement, to leave off eating animals.'
*Henry David Thoreau*

● 'I do feel that spiritual progress does demand at some stage that we should cease to kill our fellow creatures for the satisfaction of our bodily wants.'
*Mahatma Gandhi*

● 'I'm no shrinking violet. I played hockey until half of my teeth were knocked down my throat. And I'm extremely competitive on a tennis court . . . But that experience at the slaughterhouse overwhelmed me. When I walked out of there, I knew I would never again harm an animal! I knew all the physiological, economic, and ecological arguments supporting vegetarianism, but it was first hand experience of man's cruelty to animals that laid the real groundwork for my commitment to vegetarianism.'
*Peter Burwash* (champion tennis player and author of *A Vegetarian Primer)*

● 'God grant me the ability to accept the things I cannot change; the courage to change the things I can, and the wisdom to know the difference . . .'
*Old Folk Saying*

● 'The spirit in which one takes up vegetarianism is the main factor in the result. It is useless to look for any absolute proof in such matters – the proof is in one's self – for those, at least, who have heart to feel, and brain to ponder, the cruelty and folly of flesh eating. It is an issue where logic is as wholly on the one side as habit is wholly on the other, and where habit is as certainly the shield of barbarism as logic is the sword of humaneness.'
*Henry Salt*

● 'We should never begrudge money spent on food. If you do not buy the best food possible, you will pay a doctor.'
*Dr Bernard Jensen*

● 'And the flesh of slain beasts in a person's body will become his own tomb. For I tell you truly, he who kills, kills himself, and whosoever eats the flesh of slain beasts eats the body of death'.
*The Essene Gospel of Peace*

● 'Thou shalt not kill.'
*Exodus 20:13*

● 'If one pig in a million might have a chance of a contemplative lifetime instead of being skrockled up for my breakfast, it was worth swearing off meat.'
*Richard Bach*

● 'Whatever you can do, or dream you can, begin it. Boldness has genius, power and magic in it ...'
*Goethe*

● 'In the kingdom of the blind, the one-eyed man is king.'
*Old Folk Saying*

● 'As man's real power grows and his knowledge widens, ever the way he can follow grows narrower: until at last he chooses nothing but does only and wholly what he *must do*.'
*Ursula Le Guin, The Wizard of Earth Sea*

# ACKNOWLEDGEMENTS

There are many people we'd like to acknowledge for their part in making this book happen. Special thanks to Rosemary for her typing skills, Colin for the computer, Nevill for his faith and support, the staff of The Fernery for standing by us, and our customers who have let us know, through their appreciation and continuous feedback, what works and what doesn't.